"Kay Wyma is a funny, honest, and encouraging guide who will walk with you toward more peace in your life one day, one step at a time."

Holley Gerth, bestselling author of
The Powerful Purpose of Introverts

"Ultimately, everyone—irrespective of wealth, color, age, or religion—just wants to be seen, to be valued, to feel like they matter. We can do that. Kay's Peace Project invites readers to see and value people through a challenge to practice thankfulness, kindness, and mercy each day for thirty days. These practices invite humility and compassion and they open our hearts to experience humanity through the realization that we are all the same—people of great value and dignity. In doing so for others, we actually receive these things for ourselves."

Leon Logothetis, global adventurer, author, and
TV host of Netflix's *The Kindness Diaries*

"Kay shares her family's journey so openly and generously and welcomes you to the table. Grab a cup of tea or coffee and settle in as she invites you into her world in *The Peace Project*."

Melissa d'Arabian, Food Network Star, *New York Times*
bestselling author of *Ten Dollar Dinners* and *Tasting Grace*

"Without even realizing it, we develop habits of grumpiness, impatience, and suspicion. Like the force of gravity, our gaze instinctively pulls downward until we make the choice to lift our chin and look up. And when we do, everything changes. What if we decided to choose gratitude, kindness, and mercy as our consistent responses to the challenges we face every day? My friend Kay Wyma has crafted such a challenge, one this world needs right now.

"One of the things I absolutely love about Kay is how accessibly she writes and lives. As you read, you'll feel like you're riding in her car and talking to a friend. Kay's new book will simultaneously challenge you and put you in a good mood. But this is no fluff topic. When you change your gaze, when you choose to respond to life redemptively, your brain changes, your heart changes, and the world around you heals a little. Our world needs this message."

Susie Larson, talk radio host, national speaker, and author of *Fully Alive*

"Do you ever catch yourself thinking judgy thoughts about annoyances around you? Do you ever spiral down in a grumbly vortex? Me too. Oof, do I ever need this challenge. We are obsessed with monthlong challenges. Whole30, Sober October, No-Shave November, NaNoWriMo—a month can really kick-start a dream or a healthy habit. But can one month actually transform us into kinder, more merciful, more thankful people? With Kay as our guide, I think it can.

"*The Peace Project* gives us thirty days to a more gracious you. I appreciate her daily life examples. From carpool with her kids to surly people at the store, Kay shares the exasperated thoughts we all have and offers hope and helpful solutions for seeing the world through a more positive lens. Want to soothe your soul? Try *The Peace Project* and get ready to chill out."

Melanie Dale, author of *Calm the H*ck Down*

"Like a muscle in need of exercise, my soul needed *The Peace Project*. Kay and her crew tenderly led me through thirty days of practicing gratitude, kindness, and mercy. In her 'big sister' way, I felt understood while encouraged to approach everyday stresses differently. Unfortunately, I can't force others to be less rude. But thanks to Kay, I'm better equipped to control my response and find peace in any circumstance."

Heather MacFadyen, host and author of the *Don't Mom Alone* podcast and book

"What if our lives were marked with thankfulness, kindness, and mercy? Every relationship would change, perhaps none more than our marriages. If there's one thing I've learned in fifteen years of working with couples, it's that we need much more, not less, thankfulness, kindness, and mercy in our relationships. In her authentic, keep-it-real, and often humorous style, Kay Wills Wyma and *The Peace Project* help readers develop these attributes we desperately need in our most significant relationships."

Scott Kedersha, marriage pastor and author of *Ready or Knot?*

"A difference maker! *The Peace Project* gives the why and the how to change the way we approach life. Kay uses casual and relatable situations to gently offer a refreshing point of view. I immediately noticed a positive difference in my personal actions that has given me a greater, more lasting peace. Thanks, Kay."

Brenda Teele, Emmy Award–winning journalist and television personality

"Want to know the best way to change the world? Start where you are. *The Peace Project* is a soul-shifting experiment that starts with you! Grab a friend, coworker, or neighbor and follow Kay's lead. Thirty days practicing thankfulness, kindness, and mercy will leave a ripple effect of love throughout your neighborhood and community."

Kristin Schell, author of *The Turquoise Table*

the PEACE PROJECT

A 30-DAY EXPERIMENT PRACTICING THANKFULNESS, KINDNESS, AND MERCY

Kay Wills Wyma

Revell
a division of Baker Publishing Group
Grand Rapids, Michigan

Published by Revell
a division of Baker Publishing Group
PO Box 6287, Grand Rapids, MI 49516-6287
www.revellbooks.com

Printed in the United States of America

Library of Congress Cataloging-in-Publication Data
Names: Wyma, Kay Wills, author.
Title: The peace project : a 30-day experiment practicing thankfulness, kindness, and mercy / Kay W. Wyma.
Description: Grand Rapids, Michigan : Revell, a division of Baker Publishing Group, [2021] | Includes bibliographical references.
Identifiers: LCCN 2020042284 | ISBN 9780800740740 (casebound) | ISBN 9780800734787 (paperback)
Subjects: LCSH: Conduct of life. | Gratitude. | Kindness. | Mercy.
Classification: LCC BJ1531 .W96 2021 | DDC 177/.7—dc23
LC record available at https://lccn.loc.gov/2020042284

Some names and details have been changed to protect the privacy of the individuals involved.

The author is represented by the literary agency of Wolgemuth & Associates, Inc.

21 22 23 24 25 26 27 7 6 5 4 3 2 1

In keeping with biblical principles of creation stewardship, Baker Publishing Group advocates the responsible use of our natural resources. As a member of the Green Press Initiative, our company uses recycled paper when possible. The text paper of this book is composed in part of post-consumer waste.

To my mom and dad,
Sue and Don Wills,
for their seemingly endless,
always inspiring
kindness and generosity.

Contents

Foreword

Twenty years ago, at the insistence of my late wife, Debbie, I experimented with showing kindness and mercy to a homeless man known on the streets as Suicide. Though he threatened to kill me and everyone else within his reach, Suicide's aggression did not deter Debbie. She believed God spoke to her in a dream, telling her that this man possessed life-changing wisdom, and she asked me to befriend him. In the greatest leap of faith I've ever taken, after a five-month cat-and-mouse chase through our streets, this man became my friend. Who could have imagined that he would be the man God chose to show us kindness and encouragement through the darkest days of our lives?

I often wonder what would have happened had I had not taken that leap of faith and offered kindness to someone I did not believe deserved such. But this I do know: I was allowed to witness the raw power of thankfulness, kindness, and mercy in action as it worked its way into and through both of us—two very different, yet somehow the same, human beings. I watched a homeless ex-con who had never attended school a day in his life become a #1 *New York Times* bestselling author. I witnessed an angry man, known only as Suicide, become a motivational speaker. I witnessed a man who had lived by a dumpster and had been on the streets for twenty-five years become a successful artist and millionaire at age seventy-two, and then I watched him give it all away to help the poor and homeless. And he extended life-altering kindness and mercy to me, a man who he, at our meeting, did not believe deserved such. I witnessed a Black man who hated white people for most of his life become a spokesperson for racial unity with a message that it is not the color of our skin that divides us but the condition of our hearts.

What is the condition of your heart? I promise after reading this entertaining and inspiring book, your heart will be reconditioned, and everyone within your reach, and within the sound of your voice, should prepare to be blessed.

The Peace Project takes you on a journey aboard Kay's Soul30 challenge to practice thankfulness, kindness, and mercy each day for thirty days. These actions can reprogram your brain and nourish your soul. Try it and see how the world around you transforms as you practice this change of attitude and action.

Ron Hall, coauthor of the #1 *New York Times* bestselling *Same Kind of Different as Me* and *Workin' Our Way Home*

Introduction

Soul Shifting

> Isn't it odd. We can only see our outsides, but nearly everything happens on the inside.
>
> CHARLIE MACKESY

After backing out of the driveway, a morning blast of unnecessary rudeness slapped me in the face, leaving a bit of a bitter taste in my mouth. Such a lovely way to start the day.

"Really?!" I muttered. Then I sassed back with a "Well, good morning and happy day to you," even though the other driver couldn't hear me.

It all started with me in a bit of a hurry to do a grocery store quick-grab of a few forgotten items for a morning gathering at my house. I had hopped in the car and looked over my shoulder down our packed street for an opening to back out. The fact that our block dead-ends into a park means lots of cars are always parked on the street, waiting for their owners to return from the playground or leisurely strolling the path that encircles its field—which on any given day hosts football, soccer, or workout classes.

Add to the scenario a high volume of work trucks, and a swift journey down our tight street is unlikely.

This day was no different. The parked cars made it a challenge to see, but I caught a glimpse of a work truck headed my way. So I paused, and to my sweet surprise, the work truck pulled to the side and blinked its lights, inviting me to go ahead. Happy at my good fortune, I accepted the invitation and made my way into the street.

Which was about the same time a big, black pickup truck that had pulled around the paused work truck bossy-barreled up on me, staring me down until I stood down. And though the justice part of me wanted to give that truck a piece of my mind—as if there are pieces to give—I *had* to move out of the way. Which I did, navigating backwards past parked cars to squeeze into a makeshift spot, momentarily blocking someone's driveway.

As the pickup started to pass me and as I waited, tempted to glare for good measure, I was handed the opportunity to look up. Which I did. I could see the sky, bursting in beauty, the sun shining through a stunning blanket of clouds. And it was a glorious glimpse, a flash of wonder. Which is often all we get, since nature's most incredible moments disappear almost as quickly as they can be seen.

Looking up reframed the whole situation. Looking up took my eyes off myself and offered me the opportunity to see a bit beyond my moment to a much bigger picture. My heart shifted from *no-you-di'nt* indignation to compassion and thankfulness amidst a simple, though slightly begrudging, act of kindness. It was my first taste of what we would eventually call the Peace Project.

The looking up, which opened my lungs to breathe, was promptly followed by a dialing down of frustration and a firing up of gratitude. I barely had to think before a list started forming in my head.

I mean, seriously, I thought, *who cares if a suburban street standoff forced me to pull aside for a few seconds? My goodness. I'm in a car (not walking) on the way to the grocery store where fresh eggs, cold milk, frozen waffles, and countless necessities and niceties from kind people wait to be purchased.*

I took a deep breath. Add a hot summer morning to the equation (the heat fires up fast in these parts), and gratitude flows faster. *I'm blessed to be in an air-conditioned car—a car just shy of its 200K-mile mark—that is faithfully still working despite transporting our family on countless errands and trips and surviving multiple new drivers who may or may not bump a curb or possibly crash here and there.*

I could have gone on. It might seem like I am. But that's how thankfulness works. Though sometimes a challenge to start, gratitude flows easily once you get going.

As the truck accelerated by me and with my thoughts in a better place, I saw a person behind the wheel as he passed. A human being who matters. And I was reminded that you never know what's going on in someone's life. The forced pause prompted me to have compassion, to show mercy, to consider that his rush could have a reason—either he had something serious on his plate or maybe he's a jerk, either way, not great. And that flash of compassion allowed me to physically feel lighter.

Even though I was forced to pull over to let the truck through, even though I could have felt slighted, I sensed my attitude transform from frustrated to an honest please-go-first mentality. And I was floored that the entire situation could be changed by a simple mindset shift.

How and where our thoughts are anchored proves much more powerful than we may realize.

My frustration and offense were instantly dialed down and replaced with much nicer feelings of sympathy and concern. Because there may have been a real emergency. I'm sure I myself have been on the other end of an encounter like that: in a rush, not meaning to but accidentally bossing my way down a street in a mad dash.

So before moving on to the store, I sent a *this-just-happened, I'm-blown-away* message to a couple friends and got a message back almost instantly:

> Oh my gosh, that was me one time. We once made the terrible error of thinking we were close enough to the ER to just drive my son who was in extreme need of medical attention. The number of honks we got! yikes!! and so unsafe for everyone involved!!
>
> I try to remember that now as I drive when someone cuts me off or speeds by—no idea what is hidden in that back seat—but for real, we also learned to call an ambulance—LITERALLY their job.

Her words were such a terrific reminder to consider that more is at play than just our happenings. Forced kindness, a glimpse of gratitude, and a flash of mercy humanized what began as a cross encounter.

And the negative feelings that could have stolen moments out of my day—through grumbling, frustration, and such—vanished. Poof. The peace that flooded my soul was real and apparently lasting. And it made me wonder, *What could happen if I did this every day? Is the peace real?* Will *it last?*

So I asked the ladies who gathered at my house later that morning. I recounted the story, including the mutterings that ran through my thoughts and my forced-to-surrender eye roll that was so quickly displaced and replaced with feelings of calm as thankfulness, kindness, and mercy took center stage. I also told them about my *what-just-happened* wonder at the peace that had invaded my soul.

And as we sat there, I pondered out loud, "The undeniable peace I experienced was so good. A little hard to believe, but it was real."

Unafraid of silence, they paused with me.

"I mean, why wouldn't peace flood in?" a friend suggested, shrugging. "Thankfulness, kindness, and compassion pretty much line up with the greatest commandment."

I had wondered the same thing, even in the moment. "Love the LORD your God" (thankfulness), which is basically saying *eyes off me*, is followed by "love your neighbor as yourself"[1] (kindness and mercy). Why *wouldn't* peace barrel in and boss the moment?

Thankfulness shifts our eyes to the source. Then with eyes off us, even for a moment, we're able to see the person walking alongside—even a rude person—as a human being, a person of great worth, someone who matters and has dignity. All of which invites mercy, undeniably a soul-level action, as compassion takes ground and peace comes in.

I was surprised, a week later, when our group met again and someone asked to revisit the conversation. Another friend chimed in to share their own opportunity to meet rude with compassion, to find and to be grateful for all they already have rather than focusing on what they don't have. And to be kind.

Something deep and sticky had touched us. We couldn't help but continue considering the power of a simple mindset shift, wondering if the undeniable boost from a quick redirect could offer freedom in a variety of situations, regardless of age or life stage or socioeconomic standing. Offering not only freedom but also flourishing.

I'm a fan of flourishing and a huge fan of anything that will set people up for all that life offers and turn them away from the world's beatdown.

I'm not a therapist or psychological expert—unless navigating years of teen landmines with five kids makes one an expert, which it might. I'm simply a regular person with kids and friends who sometimes finds herself sucking air, a person looking to catch glimpses of the bigger picture, a person who has watched levity and freedom come forward when pressures from societal trends and messaging are dialed back.

That day on our street I could have stood my ground, forcing a stare down with the pickup. I could have even given way, pulled to the side, wallowed in the unfairness and rudeness of it all, blared my horn, and accented my displeasure with a huge stink eye. All of which, though possibly warranted, would have resulted in nothing more than bad feelings, likely coloring the rest of my day. I'm guessing I would have gone further to recount the experience to someone in my path—passing on my indignation, possibly firing it up in someone else.

What a depressing waste of time. Instead, life was breathed into the situation. Life and peace, both of which invited freedom.

That's how this soul-challenge was set into motion.

I started asking questions about the mindset shift I went through that day. What if reframing situations and circumstances *could* change the narrative? What if we could opt in to peace through acts of thankfulness, kindness, and mercy? We make time and put in effort with regard to food and exercise for our physical bodies; why not do the same for our thoughts and our souls, our innermost beings? Diets and cleanses are popular, as are exercise regimes and communities for physical fitness. Why not opt in to a regime of sorts for thought- and soul-fitness together?

"What do you guys think?" I asked my gathered friends. "Would you be game for seeing what happens if we practice thankfulness, kindness, and mercy together—and maybe track the results?"

"I'm in," one of the women replied. Which is all I needed to hear to turn an idea into a thing.

And so the Peace Project began. We all agreed to a thirty-day experiment. The perfect, or at least doable, amount of time to purposefully practice thankfulness, kindness, and mercy every day.

These practices may not be the end-all, be-all path to peace—but they certainly, powerfully, do something to invite it in and foster healthier thinking and lingering contentment. They're actions that could use some practical, everyday attention in regular life with everyday people and common situations—especially with peace and joy in play. The goodness of each is obvious, but when practiced together they're sticky—long-lasting, sometimes for days.

Inspired by the positive responses of my friends, I did what has made my family cringe in the past. I signed up and signed them up to test my hypothesis, as if I'm a scientist or sociologist who is great with numbers and tracking things. I'm almost always up for trying something that holds promise for positive life effect.

At least this time I asked.

Soul30: A Feast Rather Than a Fast

My husband, Jon, and I have five kids (ages thirteen to twenty-four) who have braved many a harebrained idea of their mother's making. Years ago, since they never asked to be a part of putting some of those ideas in print, I respected their desires for anonymity and gave them pseudonyms to share our story while respecting their privacy.

Boxster is our oldest son, followed by our girls, Snopes and Barton, then the teenage boys, Fury and Birdie. From crawling to walking, grade school to high school, with each driver's license and dorm room, my heart breaks a bit as years and stages fly by—because not only do I love these kids, I really like them. They're real, honest, forgiving, fun, and willing to talk through things with me. Every day, not all of which are full of sunshine and unicorns, I'm grateful to travel life with them.

I am also grateful for brave friends, especially this group who so kindly signed on to try my experiment and share how it changed their lives. They don't have pseudonyms, just initials. Their observations have been included "Alongside" mine throughout this book.

So with the kids and my friends on board, we committed to practice thankfulness, kindness, and mercy together for thirty consecutive days. My friends even agreed to meet once a week to share our findings and to see if peace would not only show up but linger and maybe even last. (Spoiler alert: We got more than we bargained for.)

With everything a go, I made a little logo (a simple TKM to remind us of our three practices)—somehow having something "official" made our commitment seem a bit less madcap—and started things off with basic definitions as a beginning guide.

> Thankfulness: calling out things for which to be grateful. It can be more than one thing, but not the same thing every day.
>
> Kindness: seeing and loving others (maybe ourselves too) in deed or action.
>
> Mercy: a kind or forgiving attitude toward someone that you have the power to harm or the right to punish (even ourselves).[2]

I had to do a dictionary search for a definition of mercy. Honestly, I wasn't quite sure how to define it. I had never thought much about proactively practicing mercy before, so I grabbed the first definition I saw, then modified it slightly to include "even ourselves" as we tend to be our own worst critics.

I bought nondescript journals for the kids to jot down the ways they experienced the three practices each day. Which I think they liked. Either that, or they're really nice (which they are), because they did it.

For my friends, I went a step further, offering a deeper dive into defining and understanding these practices. I put together a more substantial journal of sorts, very similar to what is compiled here, because I wanted to know more about these practices and why, when done together, the result is like a magical transport to peace. To me, if you want to know the *why,* its best to look under the hood and better understand the *what.*

What follows is a snapshot of my research, friends' testimonies noted in "Alongside" callouts, highs and lows, and honest tracking of our experiment, plus a small TKM call-to-action section that's followed by the same quote that leads each day, inviting you to jot down your own experience.

And, if simply traveling alongside to glean encouragement and possibly a few helpful tidbits here and there blesses you, great! Most everything we do is come as you are when you can. Because, more than anything, I hope you will join, maybe with a friend, in any capacity so that you might experience the freedom and peace that blooms in the process.

I was especially touched by one of my kids' willingness to sign on. He has weathered some tough things in life. From year to year, he has silently struggled—weighed down by childhood wounds. No matter the amount of proof or encouragement otherwise, thought patterns of worthlessness have become well-worn ruts for him. Before starting this experiment, I was fully aware that in our practicing thankfulness, kindness, and mercy, the hardest thing for this kid would be what he needs more than anything—mercy extended to himself. So I did my best to bridge that gap for him. That's part of what I learned along the way—that we can all bridge gaps and help each other when the task is too tough to handle alone.

Why Soul30?

Worries, pressures, and expectations face us around almost every corner in life—just like the oncoming pickup that bossed its way into my morning—threatening to hijack our thoughts.

We (our kids, our friends, and our coworkers) are almost constantly bombarded with excess messaging, information, images, spin, and more. It is hard to escape society's pressures to be beautiful, to be right, and to be successful in whatever phase of life we find ourselves. So we gear up to weather the judgment (real or perceived) that comes with it all—especially when the onslaught of negative messaging is the stuff we shower upon ourselves, a skill well-honed in the junior high years.

Gone are the days of being able to make a mistake and learn from it. There's no time. Gone are the days of enduring a blemish.

Camera-ready is no longer reserved for television personalities; everyone is on stage 24/7, 365 days a year. Gone are the days when people could agree to disagree. Chasms grow like superviruses as heels dig in and rude responses flourish, in media, in print, and through social platforms bolstered by anonymity. It can be hard to see the person on the other side of the screen when messaging is harsh, loud, and dismissive.

But newsflash: We can say no. We can stop the madness and invite in some sanity. No person should let life's heavy loads steal more joy than they already do. We can change what we spend our time thinking about and make it easier to embrace joy, laughter, and freedom at the soul-level.

We might have to fight for that mindset, but we can. And it's certainly worth the effort. And maybe even easier than we think. We can actually put into practice these simple, intentional actions of thankfulness, kindness, and mercy that feed the health of our thoughts and our souls.

Over the last several years, scientists have increased their knowledge and understanding of the human brain and its neuroplasticity. Through neuroplasticity, our thought patterns are not only changeable but they're also poised to claim new territory. New pathways form as new thought patterns present themselves. The pathways grow, taking even more territory, when supported by action. That's why the peace that comes on the other side of these practices becomes easier and easier to access.

Writer and neuroeducation researcher Daniela Silva develops research material in collaboration with New Heights Educational Group in areas related to the brain. She recently delved into the neurological impact of thought coupled with deed in her writings on kindness and the brain.

> In a practical way, every new gesture of empathy or kindness manifested by a person brings in chemical reactions between the neurons, resulting in significant changes in how the brain

> works. . . . New habits become new brain connections, and these new connections contribute to the formation of new synapses (communication between neurons), which develop in humans, new knowledge, skills and attitudes.
>
> This means that the more one practices goodness, [the] more neural connections this person will [have] in the part of the brain responsible for managing emotions. Thus, through neuroplasticity, you can convert negative thoughts and attitudes, in habits of positive behaviors, such as empathy and kindness, demystifying the idea that personality and temperament are not capable of being changed.[3]

Well-worn, life-stealing paths like fear, anxiety, frustration, insecurity, and the like can be replaced as thoughts centered on life-giving principles like thankfulness, kindness, and mercy dominate internal messaging. And when further solidified by actions (aka through practicing), new, highly traveled neuropathways take over as the superhighways for our thoughts to more easily travel.

In her article for *Health Transformer*, author Julie Hani points out psychologist Deann Ware's findings on a promising prospect: a new normal.

> When brain cells communicate frequently, the connection between them strengthens and "the messages that travel the same pathway in the brain over and over begin to transmit faster and faster." With enough repetition, these behaviors become automatic.[4]

Sounds promising, scientifically hopeful.

Through purposefully being thankful, kind, and merciful we can actively take advantage of our brain's neuroplasticity and transform our thought patterns. The idea that our thoughts travel certain paths faster and more easily than others and that we can cognitively affect those paths for the betterment of our being is exciting.

Research has shown the benefits of thankfulness, kindness, and mercy individually, but from Peace Project experience, the magic occurs when they are practiced together.

When combined, these three can gently reset the dislocation of our hearts, filling unrealized voids with peace—sometimes for days. The bounty that comes with purposefully practicing thankfulness, kindness, and mercy sits quietly in the wings throughout the day, any day, offering opportunities waiting to be tapped.

So, welcome to our less-than-perfect yet magical pilgrimage through a landscape lined with not just sightings but experiencings (I know that's not a word) of deep peace and joy on our way to what I hope is a new normal.

It's hard to describe it any other way.

DAY 1

Thankfulness: A Nice Place to Start

> We're a nation hungry for more joy; because we're starving from a lack of gratitude.
>
> BRENÉ BROWN

"I have absolutely nothing to be thankful for."

"Nothing?" I asked.

"Not one thing," a slightly crabby Birdie replied as he got in the car after school.

If this is how it's going to be, we're off to a rocky start, I thought.

When I dropped him off at school that morning, I reminded him of our new adventure. "Remember to be thankful and kind and try to show some mercy to someone," I happily chirped as he grabbed his backpack and PE bag and scrambled from the car.

"Yeah—I don't get mercy." He looked back, a little confused and possibly even annoyed at another thing to do.

"Just meet someone where they are." I searched for words as he ran out. "Okay, go for kindness."

He smiled back at me, shaking his head.

These kids are saints to put up with me. From a cookie mix business to neighborhood gatherings to taking on entitlement to carpool chats—they weather lots of my curveballs. It really isn't all bad. Some of the adventures have been fun.

I knew the on-ramp to our Soul30 challenge could be bumpy, so I had thought ahead and put Birdie's notebook in the car console earlier that day. I figured he could use the help identifying and writing things down. Plus he's so much fun to walk alongside as he contemplates life, I selfishly wanted to make sure I got to experience this thirty-day experiment with him.

So I was surprised at his response to my thankful question.

When signing everyone on for Soul30, I never imagined that calling out a thing for which to be grateful would trip anyone up. So much so, I even added a stipulation to my makeshift guidelines that every day warranted a *new* thing for which to be thankful—no repeats. Gratitude seems so easy, painless, and almost boring since it has been a cultural buzzword for the last few years.

The gratitude trend gained speed in the early 2000s along with mindfulness. Try an Amazon search for books on gratitude and you'll probably find over eighty thousand results. The idea that ticking off things for which you are thankful can change your mood seems dubious and too good to be true. But science proves it not only to be true but also good for your heart. One study from the American Psychological Association reported that practicing "gratitude was associated with better mood, better sleep, less fatigue and lower levels of inflammatory biomarkers related to cardiac health."[1]

Not only science but experience proves it as well.

A few years ago, Anna Hart, a British journalist who was researching the gratitude topic, expressed her doubt, wondering how being grateful can actually have a genuine impact. Until Brené Brown offhandedly said something to her in a phone interview.

"It's not possible to be stressed about something when you're being grateful for it."

The statement stuck with Ms. Hart, so she tried it out.

> As soon as I got off the phone to Brown, I tried it. Instead of the usual panicked thoughts (*I have so much to do*), I forced myself to be positive. "That was a thoroughly interesting interview with an incredibly smart woman," I said to myself, feeling like a loon. "Millions of Oprah-watching Americans would give their right hand to speak to her. What a treat! And now I get to whittle it into an article and make her insights accessible to thousands of readers! Could today get any better?"

Her words might sound hokey, but they produced results.

> Thinking gratefully worked. Right away. Suddenly my day ahead wasn't littered with obstacles, it was a trail of treats. I knew I was tricking myself, like a small child being told to play a new game of "tidy up the playroom." But knowing that didn't stop it working, and in 10 years of researching and writing about social trends and popular psychology, this was the first time I'd been genuinely amazed.
>
> I began using the technique in other areas of my life. . . . It was exhilarating to find a simple technique that had the power to change how I felt about the day ahead, the person next to me, and my current life circumstances.[2]

Honestly, I felt the same way as Ms. Hart. Doubtful, then amazed. Hers has been our experience too. *Still* it seems we first must get to the willingness part of practicing thankfulness, which can sometimes be the hardest part.

That first step involves letting go of whatever has our mind trapped in stubborn ingratitude. If we can't, then we probably need to dutifully take steps away from being focused on ourselves by ticking off specific things for which to be thankful, whether we believe it will work or not.

At least my front seat passenger was honest.

One of my favorite (and not-so-favorite) things about walking life alongside tweens and teenagers has to be the raw authenticity with which questions—especially those lobbed during a car ride—are answered.

I quit running carpool with other people years ago. Even though convenience flies out the window, opportunities to genuinely communicate abound in the car. Maybe it's because we're seat belted in place, or maybe it's because we aren't looking at each other. I don't know. And *abound* may be an overstatement, but the opportunities exist—with great regularity. And that is something to be said since such conversations are like tiny gold finds, diamond chips in the rough. Raw authenticity during a time in life when flight (as in, to your room to be alone and self-obsess) usually wins out against fight (as in, to see reality rather than all the ridiculousness societal messaging throws your way).

But I didn't do a good job of meeting my gratitude-deficient kid in his funk. No, I entered with my own. Who knew? I guess it had been a long day for me too.

"Really, nothing? Nothing to be thankful for?" I asked.

I took a breath, gathering a list to hit him with since I had just left my second funeral in two days. The day before, I attended a funeral celebrating a life cut short by cancer, leaving behind a loving husband and a four-year-old son. That day, I was returning from a funeral celebrating a life ended by someone who just couldn't take it anymore, leaving behind a family who would have given anything for him to have believed his worth.

So I went there—I blasted Birdie with a whole slew of gratitude reminders.

"I can tell you some things you can be thankful for," I began. "Lots of things. I'm dressed up because I had a funeral today. You can be grateful we're alive; grateful you have a family that loves you. You have teachers who know your name; you get to go to school; you have a mother who is sitting right next to you, able to touch you and tell you out loud I love you."

I looked over at Birdie, who had passed from wide-eyed listening to the beginnings of silent tears. And I stopped. Suddenly I wished I hadn't started.

"Why would you say those things to me?" he choked out while swallowing a sob. "Don't you know that my greatest fear is being without you?"

Okay—so that really backfired.

I pulled over, and took another deep breath. This time, I grabbed hold of mercy.

Birdie's a middle school boy who likely spent the day being peppered with insecurity, likely solidified by other middle school kids who were dealing with their own insecurities. Let alone all the performance/peer pressures and intensities kids face these days. My goodness, why not meet my son in his funk rather than wallow in mine?

I looked him straight in the eye. "You are right. I am SO sorry."

And I prayed for him to extend mercy to me as I apologized, because he *was* right. I shouldn't have handed him a load of my heavy day that offered everything but an opportunity for gratitude. He's a kid. And he's in a phase of life that's plagued by thoughts of insufficiency, especially when compared to lists of do's and be's that bring endless opportunities to come up on the short end of inevitable comparison to everyone else.

I apologized for what had to have felt like being hit with a bat. I honestly and compassionately met him where he was. I was hoping that he could hear me and understand and find the solid ground. It was there. Believe it or not, solid ground is always there. And I prayed that he could hold on to the truth that he is loved, that I'm not going anywhere, and that if/when I do, he will be okay.

I fought to grab hold of mercy for myself. Because in moments like these, we need to be understanding and kind to ourselves. Sometimes we find ourselves with short fuses or empty tanks because a day has been long. For me, those things were heavy on my mind because I was sad and a bit tired. Tired of illness and tired of flat-out lies about worth and identity that steal our days. I was tired of pressures and people that would steal from my kid's day.

And in that fatigue, I started a rant and spewed a list of things for which to be grateful, sure—but a list that the check in my heart warned was too heavy for him and probably for me.

"Sweetheart," I began again, "I know you've probably had a long day. Apparently I have too. And long days can make it hard to be grateful. I shouldn't have pressed. All I can do is ask for forgiveness."

I paused, then added, "I really am sorry." Because on long days, gentleness can go a long way.

"It's okay." He smiled at me.

I smiled back. And we both breathed. We were still pulled over.

"Mom?"

"Yes?"

"This is getting a bit awkward. Can we go?"

Grateful for his forgiveness and humor, I started the car and we headed for home.

We hadn't gone far when he looked at me. "I *am* grateful for you," he said. "*And* I'm grateful for Ms. Begert and art. I'm grateful for this car because walking home would be long and hot." Then with a sweet gleam in his eye, this time not from tears, he added, "I think we should celebrate our not-walking with a stop at McDonald's."

He said it just in time for us to turn into the drive-through, which I did, happily.

Mercy, even the tiny bit of mercy in that moment, did what it seems to do; it invited freedom. Mercy given and received.

But for mercy to ignite, it must be invited into the conversation and accessed, literally activated by calling it into the process with genuine hearts willing to be humble and ready to receive.

Because whether we are having mercy upon someone else or upon ourselves, we always experience freedom. Another thing for which to be thankful.

Interestingly enough, gratitude isn't just an easy place to start or simply a passenger along for the ride; it's guiding our drive. Thankfulness primes the pump for kindness and mercy to flow.

ALONGSIDE

THANKFULNESS: Unexpected Benefits

I just am not a merciful person. I don't have the patience. I can't tell you how many times I've told my kids or friends to get over it. I mean, really.

So it surprised me that within days of starting the Peace Project, my pausing to call out thankfulness then choosing compassion actually invited mercy, which I didn't think I had. And it made me feel more connected to my son.

My extending mercy made him nicer—and me too.

When I came at this issue with compassion, seeing things that could be hard for him, it made me (us all, really) surprisingly patient with others.

My reaching for mercy in a situation where I would normally have scoffed at it dialed everything down. I think my son felt heard. Which I didn't know he felt otherwise. And our day was better—even hours later.

I don't know if it will happen again, but who knew it could?

—LM—

TKM How have you practiced?
What have you learned?

We're a nation hungry for more joy; because we're starving from a lack of gratitude.

BRENÉ BROWN

DAY 2

Be Brave, Be Kind

> Kindness is the language which the deaf can hear and the blind can see.
>
> MARK TWAIN

"Is Steve Hartman on this one?" Snopes asked, moving a couple of pillows to sit down next to me on the couch.

It was an early Saturday morning. We're usually the only ones awake. I had already made a donut run for the boys and grabbed a few Bubba's breakfast biscuits for us while I was out. We were on day 2 of our pilgrimage—at least that's how Snopes referred to it—and we were on the hunt for kindness as it inspires kindness.

We get hit by so much negative information these days, but Steve Hartman, on CBS's *Sunday Morning*, consistently finds and shares stories that offer a reminder that kindness and goodness are in the midst—equally, if not abundantly, around us. Just often unsung.

That particular morning Steve hit a home run. In fact, Snopes and I found ourselves fighting back tears as he shared the impact of the simplest act of kindness. The segment was about a young boy named Finn who has Down Syndrome and is on the autism spectrum.

Finn is enamored by the American flag. His parents say that his unique challenges are what have allowed him to have such a deep appreciation for the flag. Honestly, how many times have any of us slowed down and gazed at the physical symbol of our freedom? Finn does—every time he sees it. His dad thinks it's the flag's movement in the wind that really captures Finn's attention.

When he sees the flag, Finn will sit for an hour or more, simply watching it sway, lost in the motion that appears to bring him comfort, even contentment. Finn is especially mesmerized by a flag along his walk that belongs to a neighbor named Todd Disque. One day Todd noticed Finn lingering at his tree upon which his flag proudly waves. And he acted. Todd took the extra steps beyond just thinking about what might bless Finn to actually doing a simple and kind yet deeply impactful act.

Moved by the boy's wonder, he went to work to make Finn's stay a little more enjoyable. Todd built a makeshift bench, a place for Finn to sit. "Nothing fancy," he said. He just "sawed some boards and made a little perch for that little patriot." And he didn't make a big deal or present any fanfare. "He just left it out by the tree for Finn's family to discover."

Which Finn did and does. He now sits and lingers and enjoys.

Simple kindness.

Beautiful.

Finn's parents see the bench as a symbol of the goodness in humanity. It's a reminder that "there's still good people out there that want to do kind things for no other reason than just to be kind."[1]

To be kind with no ulterior motive, no effort to self-promote but simply to care for another human in life, is powerful. Such action requires a significant amount of bravery. Because you never know how someone might react. They could be offended or put off because not everyone is open to receiving good things. In fact, rejection sometimes comes on the other side of kindness.

It happened to me the other day when my attempt to offer a hand up to a stranger was met with a lovely barrage of how my help wasn't needed or wanted. It was even topped off with a few expletive-laden directions on where I could go. I'm not going to lie; those words stung. But thankfully mercy was close by, standing ready to gently diffuse my own defensive response with compassion reminders of the hurt that must be a part of that person's world. Soul-wounds were visibly apparent in the crusty wall he had built to insulate and isolate himself. My heart broke as mercy flooded the entire situation. And my attempted act of kindness morphed from a meal to a gentle response filled with understanding (to the best of my ability) and respect alongside a genuine prayer that he might someday know his value and worth.

In offering kindness simply to be kind, with nothing to get in return, sometimes we put ourselves out there. In fact, an offering of kindness may be as far as we get. But even an offer is something. It's a reminder that someone can be and is seen.

All acts of kindness, whether received or rejected, are courageous and can change the world. Because at the core, when fueled by gratitude and buttressed by compassion, caring for another human is powerful. Such actions hold the type of power that moves mountains. It's the type of power that is a double-edged sword, cutting both ways—not harming but leveling barriers and inviting peace for all the parties involved. It's a power that lingers in the same way that Finn lingers in peace and contentment, mesmerized by the rhythmic motion of a moving flag.

Acts of kindness are like taking supervitamins that empower and keep empowering much longer than the act itself. Not all acts of kindness come in the form of a semipermanent bench, a physical reminder of goodness. But they do all come with undeniable uplifting. Even, maybe especially, the silent acts that go without recognition.

There's even scientific support showing the incontestable positive effects on our brains that occur when we practice kindness.

Psychologists at the University of Sussex found that there are two types of kindness that affect our brains in different ways. One involves getting something in return for doing a kind act ("strategic"); the other expects nothing in return ("altruism"). And scans show they both have different impacts on the brain.

> When you're being strategic, the striatal regions of the brain, which give feelings of reward, light up, and you get a rush of positive feelings.[2]

Which is good. But even better . . .

> Altruism, the scientists found, lights up a whole spectrum of the brain. It uses the striatal areas too, but it also activates the subgenual anterior cingulate cortex, which is involved in our mood, making us happy. Another area that shows a lot of activity when we're being generous? The ventromedial prefrontal cortex, which affects our decision-making and is a crucial part of making empathetic decisions that bond us to others.[3]

According to the study's authors, "it seems there is something special about situations where our only motivation to give to others is to feel good about being kind."[4]

It's kindness simply to be kind.

How interesting to learn that strategic kindness, which expects something in return (eyes on me), only goes so far. But altruistic kindness, with eyes off ourselves and onto others, packs a much more significant punch.

We can get so caught up in rudeness, thinking it rules the world these days, especially since it grabs most headlines. But on the whole, people are nice. Regular people, far from famous, driving next to us, living normal days lined with good and bad, are nice. And in nice people, kindness abounds.

Physically we flourish when we are kind.

Practicing kindness releases endorphins (natural painkillers), and it elevates levels of dopamine, prompting what is called a "helper's high" as pleasure regions of the brain light up. "Kindness improves mood, depression and anxiety. Kindness stimulates the production of serotonin which heals wounds, calms and increases happiness."[5]

But that's not all. "People who practice kindness as a habit have 23 percent less cortisol (the stress hormone) and more of a chemical called nitric oxide, which dilates blood vessels, thus lowering blood pressure."[6]

Not only is practicing kindness worth a try but daily exercise can form a habit and become second nature. This healthy practice was heralded by Christ as part of the greatest commandments. He didn't tout it as another task to do in order to live up to expectations or as a shaming indictment but as an on-ramp to joy and peace.

Even hearing about Todd's act of true kindness toward Finn made Snopes and I physically feel good. We were inspired, an emotion that involves our thoughts. Yet the deeper impact of kindness comes when our thoughts move to action and become experience. Opportunities to practice kindness are everywhere.

I watched it come into play later that evening as Birdie got in the car after a small group gathering.

"How was it?" I lobbed his way.

"Well," he sighed, "I had decided to be crabby. I didn't want to go. But you made me, so I decided to hold on to some leftover crabby from yesterday." Yes, we know that things hadn't gone his way the day before when he and I shared the heavy list of gratitude reminders. "But truth be told," he continued, "I had a great time. And honestly, it all started when I noticed Sam was standing alone, so I asked him if he wanted to come play ping-pong."

"It's hard being the new kid," he continued. "I get that. So I really wanted to help him out. And that was that—the crab was gone."

Hilarious. Who plans crabbiness? Apparently tweenagers. Well, and full-blown teenagers. And now that we're talking about it, sometimes their sisters, brothers, and maybe even their moms.

But even in planned crabbiness, kindness stands ready to come and save the day.

ALONGSIDE

KINDNESS IN ACTION: Carpool Drop-Off Lines

I get it. We are all in a hurry to get to work or to the next drop-off. I have the luxury of walking my kids to school. Today I watched a mom get out of her car and encourage her sweet boy (probably a kinder or first grader) to go to class. He did not want to go. Today was picture day, so he was all dressed up and looking fine.

His mom had to quickly get back in her car, so I walked beside him and started a conversation (mostly me talking) as we slowly headed into school. At one point, he looked back, saying, "Mama?" But I told him I would walk him in because his mom had to get to work.

We got through the front doors and up to the next set of double doors that lead to the classrooms. He started backing up, not wanting to go in. The school nurse and I talked to him about how great he looked and what a fun day it would be. Then another student, dressed in her finest with hair too gorgeous for words, walked up next to the little boy and said, "Come on, Sam, let's go to class."

She gently put her arm around him, patted him on the back, and they walked down the hallway to class together.

THIS IS KINDNESS!

Little did I know, this sweet boy has special needs. If I had judged his mom for getting out of the car in the drop-off line or for walking him up to the walkway, I would have missed an opportunity to see God's heart at work in the lives of a mom, a school nurse, and a classmate.

Everyone has a story! BE BRAVE. BE KIND.

—BF—

TKM How have you practiced?
What have you learned?

Kindness is the language which the deaf can hear and the blind can see.

MARK TWAIN

DAY 3

Mysterious Mercy

> The name of God is mercy. There are no situations we cannot get out of, we are not condemned to sink into quicksand.
>
> POPE FRANCIS

By day 3 of the Peace Project, the kids had already handed me the mercy card, even though the concept was still new to us.

And honestly, I was grateful.

Pulling up to a cross street, I was driving with them all in the car. The guy stopped at the light in front of us just sat there, even though the light had changed to green. It's a neighborhood street, so we were all fully aware that the light stays green for—on a good day—five seconds.

"GO!" I urged the car. "PLEASE GO! For goodness' sake, we're trying to make a movie on time," I pleaded with the driver, as if he could hear me.

The car slowly moved forward as the light turned yellow.

"Oh my gosh!" I might have even thrown up my arms. "What in the world is that person thinking?"

"Mercy," someone said from the back seat.

"Yeah, Mom—mercy," echoed another.

"Ahh." I sighed. Be careful what you ask from those around you. "You're right," I relented. "Who knows what's going on in his life. Even if he was just on his phone, maybe he needed a mental break. Or if he's distracted by a bad day—whatever, it's okay. Wow." I sighed again. I sure was quick to get frustrated. A little slow to get on the mercy train—even though I knew it's a better ride than being frustrated.

"Yeah, Mom," one of them said. They all laughed.

Then another added, "Glad *you're* not Jesus."

Hysterical.

Oh my word. I'm glad too. I would choose his unending, ever-present mercy over mine any (every!) day.

I'm humbled and grateful that the people with whom I walk life care and are willing to call me and each other out, earnestly, not in a gotcha sort of way. I'm grateful for laughter—the gentle way it brings levity and the way it invites mercy into the conversation.

I think we have all realized that mercy is both the most difficult and the most deeply moving aspect of this exercise. It seems to hit our soul's core, working from the inside out.

Mercy is not about condoning but about redeeming. It's about counteracting and correcting something negative—to make good something gone wrong. It's about dignity—the worth of a human being. Actually, all the people involved are touched when mercy comes into play.

Mercy, according to the Oxford Dictionary, means "a kind or forgiving attitude toward someone that you have the power to harm or the right to punish,"[1] to which we've added "even ourselves."

James Keenan, a Jesuit priest, calls mercy "the willingness to enter into the chaos of another,"[2] which I find a remarkable interpretation, especially as it references the *chaos*—the noise and all that comes with it—*of another*. Whether the chaos is history (as in, personal history peppered with all sorts of good and bad incidents) or happenings in a day or even the flurry in our thoughts, whatever has taken center stage and somehow invaded our space comprises our own chaos. Which is about the time when things can get complicated.

I like that Keenan's definition starts with humility. It seems like a humble heart is key to enacting mercy's magic, like yeast to dough.

Willingness is the humble action point of mercy's compassion. *Willingness* comes from a place of solid ground, where our worth has been determined and our identity defined. Because mercy at its core has nothing to do with us being powerless, a victim. Just the opposite, it has everything to do with our operating from a solid sense of worth—the only place from which genuine compassion can rise. Willingness invites compassion and grace (mercy components), so we can see a person as a human being and all that comes with that. It's never victimization.

Already on our Soul30 pilgrimage, we each had struggled with practicing mercy. Mercy is not a one-and-done thing. In fact, the same mercy opportunities tend to keep arising—which likely invite a peek behind the curtain to see our need to address old wounds, frustrations, stubborn bitterness, and other things we've packed away in hopes of avoidance.

Practicing mercy has brought into the conversation the absolute necessity of healthy boundaries so that mercy can do what it does—redeem. It's not about handing over our dignity so that a person or situation can bully us into some perverted submission. It's actually about claiming dignity.

Mercy replaces frustration, judgment, resentment, and such with hope and grace. And all these things act as an on-ramp for the peace that comes with them.

In her book *The Choice*, Dr. Edith Eva Eger offers some insight into mercy, though she doesn't name her experience as such. At the age of sixteen, Edith, a prisoner at Auschwitz, found herself face-to-face with Holocaust doctor Josef Mengele, the notorious "Angel of Death"—a truly sick individual who used his power to dehumanize, abuse, and murder thousands of people.

A "refined killer and lover of the arts," he pulled Edith, a known accomplished dancer, from the larger group of prisoners to perform for him. She recounts:

> As I dance, I discover a piece of wisdom that I have never forgotten. I will never know what miracle of grace allows me this insight. It will save me many times, even after the horror is over. I can see that Dr. Mengele, the seasoned killer who just this morning murdered my mother, is more pitiful than me. I am free in my mind, which he can never be. He will always have to live with what he's done. He is more a prisoner than I am. As I close my routine with a final, graceful split, I pray, but it isn't myself I pray for. I pray for him. I pray, for his sake, that he won't have the need to kill me.[3]

Yes, mercy is not victimhood. No one is making anyone a victim or condoning victimization, especially not victimizing ourselves, by showing mercy to others. Mercy actually offers freedom by tapping into the mysterious power of forgiveness that involves acknowledging wrongdoing—not condoning it—and heading off bitterness at the pass with the "willingness to enter into the chaos of another."

I told Snopes about James Keenan's definition the other day.

"What an interesting way to think about it," she said.

"Isn't it?" I nodded in response. And we both paused—I guess quietly considering what it looks like to willingly enter someone else's chaos. After a moment, I said, "I think compassion and forgiveness have to be added to the end of the sentence."

"Yeah," Snopes agreed. "Maybe that's where willingness starts—with compassion and forgiveness, or maybe simply one or the other by themselves. Do you think?"

"Seems like it. Compassion sure is easier than forgiveness to grab in the moment. Maybe we will find out as we go." Because at the core soul-level, that's exactly what God, who is "compassionate and gracious . . . slow to anger and abounding in love and faithfulness"[4] did for us—he forgave and he loved.

Staggering.

Saint Francis of Assisi, an Italian Catholic friar, was known for mercy. In fact, his contemplation of it and wonder at its power earned him the label "channel of mercy." He embraced, experienced, and took note of mercy's transformational power as it affected the core level of his soul. Mercy softened and deeply altered him—setting him free from preconceived ideas and perceptions and setting him on a path toward connection with people, even people he had once thought wretched.

In his *Testament,* he shared about his time serving people he did not want to serve and the way his heart transformed as he did:

> It seemed too bitter for me to see lepers. And the Lord Himself led me among them and I *showed mercy* to them. And when I left them, what had seemed bitter to me was turned into sweetness of soul and body. And afterwards I delayed a little and left the world.[5]

In an article on how this played out, Brian Purfield of the Mount Street Jesuit Center said that Francis, while on his deathbed, "understood that his story began with an encounter with a human being, one who was looked upon with horror and disgust: the leper."[6] He went on to explain,

> Lepers were excluded from society and were abhorred by people. By starting his story at this point, Francis gives us a key to his spiritual outlook: if you are looking to discover God, look for the leper in your life, the person who is most troubling to you.
>
> Francis tells us what he did in that encounter with the leper: he acted with *misericordia*—mercy or, more accurately translated, with a heart sensitive to misery. . . . He entered into the chaos of the lepers' lives. Not only are *their* lives changed, but Francis' life takes on a new direction. He is converted from fear of them to love of them. A new story begins.[7]

I wonder, Will practicing kindness and mercy with a *heart sensitive to misery* provide a new beginning for all who live by them? Will they begin *our* new story?

Already we're discovering that in the action piece of kindness and mercy, especially mercy, "sweetness of the soul and body" do abound—and peace gently invades our innermost being.

Mercy is a narrative changer.

Whether it's the internal conversations we have with ourselves concerning ourselves—you know, the messaging on how we fall short when everyone else measures up, or all life's *shoulds*, *woulds*, and *coulds*—or concerning the chaos of others, mercy stands poised and ready to rescue, to redeem.

The power in practicing thankfulness, kindness, and mercy was just beginning to be realized around our home. Though most of us have not served lepers like Saint Francis of Assisi nor have we shared Dr. Eger's past of coming face-to-face with a horrific murderer, we too can tap into mercy's deep well of peace as we reach for compassion and push aside misgivings or bitterness. Not in some grand fell swoop but step-by-step.

Thirty days might not be enough.

ALONGSIDE

MERCY: In Office Hallways

I woke up this morning with the question, What will mercy do today?

Today I choose to extend mercy to people in my past, to replace bitterness with kindness, and to thank God for the feast.

Because that's what this process feels like—a feast of goodness. So much so, I actually stopped myself from participating in office chatter about a colleague who had absolutely annoyed many in the group. I certainly had something to add, but I kept my mouth shut—fighting my thoughts to land on forgiveness rather than stirring the pot.

The craziest thing? I physically felt better than if I had jumped into the mix. And it wasn't just for a moment I felt better; the lightness lasted.

When I passed that colleague later that day, I could freely greet her without bitterness and with genuine care—all while respecting boundaries.

Compassion isn't always a call to enter into a minefield. But if we are to enter, go only *after* it has been swept—apparently with mercy.

—BT—

TKM How have you practiced?
What have you learned?

The name of God is mercy. There are no situations we cannot get out of, we are not condemned to sink into quicksand.

POPE FRANCIS

DAY 4

No Small Act

> Remember, there is no such thing as a small act of kindness. Every act creates a ripple with no logical end.
>
> SCOTT ADAMS

Racing for the door and then into the car, we all said a quick prayer of thankfulness. Birdie had just averted a wardrobe malfunction, and after his disastrous wardrobe issues the week before, the relief from the near miss alone could have bolstered any day.

The previous week's clothing snafu began in the morning carpool line with a gasping-for-air realization that things were not well in our world.

"Why is Braeden wearing a blazer?" I asked Birdie as we pulled up to the drop-off spot after noticing a few of his friends' outfits as they walked into school.

"And long pants," Birdie noted.

Squinting to see the lay of the land, together we tried to stuff those terrible, horrible feelings of dread that bubble to the surface the moment you begin to realize that something very important has quite possibly been overlooked. That feeling when the school number pops up on caller ID or when you realize that you've forgotten to be somewhere or to study for a test.

I know this feeling. On more than one occasion, because I'm calendar-challenged, I've eyed a phone number and wondered, *Who could be calling me from . . . ?* and my mind races through places I should be or people I might have forgotten. I *am* that person who has sat down in a college classroom and answered questions like "Did you study?" with "Study for what?" as a major exam is passed my way. Which is really the tip of the iceberg for me amid forgetfulness and managing lots of moving parts.

My poor family. I like to think that weathering all my curveballs has made them flexible, maybe even stronger. It has absolutely increased their capacity to extend grace and mercy as they've had so much practice with their mom.

So as Birdie and I surveyed the morning drop-off, where shorts are the standard go-to every other day, reality began to set in. Seeing more blazers and long pants, he took a deep breath while watching everyone (actually, *everyone*) walk into school properly dressed.

"School pictures," we said in tandem, with dread. Even though there had been plenty of reminders, both of us had forgotten that school pictures, which required proper attire, were that day.

"Okay." I looked over at him in the few seconds we had remaining before he had to disembark. "I'll run home and look for a blazer. You head in and see if you can find a pair of pants in the lost and found."

My mind started racing. *Surely we have a blazer at home that will fit. He has two older brothers who certainly have had need for a blazer—though I usually borrow rather than buy such items. We can still hope. Just like we can hope a stray pair of pants has made its way to the lost and found box, because I know we don't have those. And that box is always overflowing.*

Yes. This is us. Keeping it real, people.

The great thing—upon arriving home and running upstairs, I *did* find a blazer, which I grabbed and raced back to school and snuck into his locker. Another great thing—he found pants. The bad thing—the pants, the only available pair, were sized to fit an eight-year-old. He's thirteen.

But he did it. And he owned it.

My goodness. As if I didn't have enough respect for this amazing kid. He rocked that pair of tiny pants. The mid-shin pedal pushers might have passed on a beach somewhere, but in the school halls, they caught a few glances. He couldn't button them, so he pulled the zipper as close to the top as possible. Then he creatively used his belt to hold them together, positioning his shirt with just the right amount of untucking to cover their unavoidable openness. He wore them like this—the *entire* day. For some strange reason, individual and class pictures occurred at different times on the same day, so he walked the halls and somehow sat through classes, rising to the occasion with his head held high.

Upon picking him up, we laughed about it all. "How did you do it?" I asked, my jaw dropping at the sight of those tiny pants.

"I could barely breathe for most of the day. But it was okay." He loosened the belt and let the zipper fall as he took a deep breath and exhale-sighed with relief. "Of course, Chuck had to call it out in first period. He literally pointed at me and laughed and said 'Hey, Baby Pants.' I just looked at him and shook my head, which seemed enough."

"You're amazing," I said in awe. Seriously.

So when Birdie averted another wardrobe malfunction the next week—this time a shirt on inside out and a downed zipper, thankfully caught *before* getting out the door—he happily relished in his good fortune.

We had only just started down the road of practicing thankfulness, kindness, and mercy, but already something indisputable was happening. Granted, it could have been the newness of it all. Like the initial euphoria that occurs when a starter pistol goes off and the first mile feels great in a race. But something longer-lasting appeared to be happening. (And, thankfully, no running was required.)

Before discovering the inside-out shirt and downed zipper, Birdie had already gotten his brother's breakfast for him, quietly and with no fanfare. Happily, proactively helping out as if it were early-morning business as usual. Maybe it was an overflow of good feelings from the last couple of days—the kindness he had been extending, the reluctant gratitude that lightened his load—but his proactive effort was undeniable.

And the kindness didn't stop there.

"Oh no," Fury moaned from the back seat when we were halfway to school.

"What is it?" I asked, looking at the clock to make sure we were on time. He doesn't like being late.

"It's nothing." He resign-sighed.

"No, really?" I asked, urging him to share. These kids are genuinely fine human beings. They are nice and don't like to burden anyone, which is great but not always necessary since their burdens can often be easily solved.

"I forgot the money I need for a book," he said. He actually hadn't forgotten. He remembered at home while eating breakfast. We scrambled to find a twenty-dollar bill, which we did, but he accidentally left it on the counter as we raced out the door.

"Oh, honey," I joined in his sigh. "That's no problem. Let's look around in the car."

Our car has been known to hide all sorts of helpful items. Usually a stray pair of shoes in case you forgot yours. Socks, pencils, a math textbook, and sometimes money. We rarely find bills, but the coins add up. Because, yes, you can pay for gas with coins. I've been there, scavenged, and done it—once or twice in pajamas. But no need to go there, especially since, on this morning, we found nothing.

"Okay." We were stopped at a light, so I turned to look at both the boys. "We have a choice here—"

"No, it's not a problem, Mom," Fury protested, ready to live with the consequence of not getting his required book.

"Wait," I objected, "we really have a choice. I have my bank card. We can easily run by and get money for the book. It's not that far out of the way."

"Yes!" Birdie chimed in. "That's a great idea. Do that. And drop him off first, then take me. He's on the way, and I'm fine with that."

Fury again protested, not wanting anyone to suffer for his sake. Because truth be told, we each knew that a detour—even a small one—would likely set into motion a school tardy.

Birdie insisted. "I've got nothing going on. And if we go now, I think we can make it to both schools on time."

Fury conceded, mostly because I conceded for him. The bank was close. There was no line, so it only took a minute to get the money he needed. We dropped him off and, without an ounce of stress, made our way to Birdie's school.

Pulling into the drop-off line, we looked at the clock. He was tardy.

Birdie chuckled, I guess remembering the stress of driving up on the school picture day. "Thank goodness we noticed the shirt and zipper *before* getting to school!" He laughed, then without a care in the world about being tardy added, "It's already a good day."

His nonchalance made me wonder if the morning's act of kindness prompted his thoughts to travel to thankfulness rather than frustration. Mercy had invaded our morning scene. Birdie entered Fury's chaos, not as a victim but with compassion and understanding. He had sympathy for his brother—his finding money, forgetting money, possibly being without a required book, the potential embarrassment and/or consequence. He didn't get mad, not even for a second, when he was the one late for school due to the extra detour.

And as crazy as it is, Birdie didn't get out of the car afraid or embarrassed by being late. His tank was already filled and overflowing with the peace that comes from seeing and leaning into compassion, from showing genuine care and love for the people in his life. Then, even more amazingly, when I picked him up from school (remember: middle school!), his tank was still full.

Mercy was at the core of it all.

I'm not sure why practicing kindness is so powerful, but I think mercy with its compassion and deep soul connection has something to do with it.

Practicing thankfulness and kindness tills the ground, inviting a gentle response and a positive attitude, which in turn helps us to genuinely practice mercy—possibly the most powerful practice of our Peace Project. Absolutely the most mysterious.

ALONGSIDE

KINDNESS AND MERCY: Small Is Big

It is interesting to me how sometimes it's the insignificant things, the simple things we don't think matter, that are what allow us or free us to show compassion or to be kind in the big things.

Sometimes it's easy for me to think, *I really want a big thing by which to show mercy or kindness.* But I think it's interesting how, like in the car, it's these little things that prime the pump for when we really need it.

—DR—

TKM How have you practiced?
What have you learned?

Remember, there is no such thing as a small act of kindness.
Every act creates a ripple with no logical end.

SCOTT ADAMS

DAY 5

Mercy's Soul Sightings

> Gratitude magnifies the spirit and promotes well-being. In good times and bad, authentic appreciation creates perspective, literally stepping back from the distractions of the moment and affirming something more lasting than passing circumstance.
>
> ERIC MOSLEY AND DEREK IRVINE

Walking into the kitchen, I couldn't help but smile. There on the coffee maker sat my credit card, directly on top of the button I would soon be pressing in order to brew a delicious cup of yummy goodness to start my day.

It's the little things in life—some that are actually larger than life—that are so easily overlooked but worth the pause.

Which is what I did. I paused to consider (with gratitude) life's small pleasures, like a hot cup of coffee. And I thanked God for the kid I had handed that card to the night before so he could take his friend to the movie. This kid who has already experienced some deep heartache in his young life. This kid who, despite almost incessant feelings of worthlessness, is one of the kindest people I know.

His simple act of kindness flooded me with warmth and made me feel known and loved. I'm sure he wasn't going for that, but I was and am thankful for him. He knows me well enough that he put my card right where I would see it in the morning. And I lingered for a moment in how good it felt to be known.

Being known, accepted, and loved are core human needs that, if left unmet, silently chip away at our soul, leaving us sorely lacking.

Recently, through a broadcast from London, a National Health Service psychiatrist named Dr. Chi Chi Obuaya shared something he learned while attending a conference. A fellow doctor from the US named Ned Hallowell stressed "the importance of Vitamin C and how that sustains us." But not Vitamin C as we might understand it. No, in this instance "the *c* stands for connection," Dr. Obuaya said as he urged people to be intentional in connecting with others during these times of isolation caused by the COVID-19 pandemic.[1]

Humans are made for connection. Relationship is woven within us. The need doesn't go away, regardless of age, circumstance, or socioeconomic environment. It's a common ground, human condition we all share simply because we're people. We *need* connection.

One place I especially love to watch connection is at the Laundromat—it's the great equalizer.

I love the Laundromat. I recently visited our go-to, the Spin Cycle, when our dryer decided to take a break. Or maybe just *break*.

The Laundromat is your friend. You can get done in an hour what normally takes all day. And rather than wash, let sit, wash again (please tell me we're not the only ones), dry, wait, fluff, wait, fluff, fold since more loads need the dryer, you can get it all done at once.

The Laundromat is amazing. I can run four washing machines and six dryers at the same time and complete what seems to be a never-ending task in less than two hours.

And the *people* at the Laundromat are terrific. Not just the staff but also the patrons. Well, most of them. There was one guy who tried to sell me used television parts as I shuffled in trying to balance my load. When I declined the deal, he then shot me the standard "can you spare two dollars for my bus ride?" I'm not saying he was spinning a story, but he had been sitting and chatting with everyone until he saw me and any other fresh meat who walked through the door. But even in his press for cash, he was still so nice.

I think the Laundromat is like the eighties sitcom *Cheers* "where everybody knows your name." While I was putting coins in my washer, a guy walked in and, as if on cue, the core group seated at the tables that lined the front of the Spin Cycle chimed in together, "Freddie!!" Pleasantries, winks, and back-slap embraces were exchanged as he grabbed a cart and started to sort.

The common denominator: people. Human beings doing what we do. All ages, all colors, all demographics. One guy was reading his *Economist* and sipping a Starbucks. Another guy sat chewing through a bag of Sour Patch Kids while mindlessly watching his towels fall over each other in the dryer. TVs blared Spanish and English with *Dora the Explorer* winning out on volume. No one cares about the program of choice because we all respect the moms in need of a distraction for their little ones who can only take so much watching machines spin.

The Laundromat is for everyone. Because *everyone* has dirty clothes. Everyone has to wash them. Everyone dries. Everyone sorts and folds. Everyone searches for matching socks. (Some of us more than others.)

If we can get past life's hectic racing and competition enough to slow down and look around, we might be able to see people who are just like us, even though they might look or sound different. People who go through challenges. People who celebrate successes. People who have a history. People with hopes and dreams, with heartaches and hardship. Creative people, bright people, funny people, extroverts, and introverts.

As I stood next to a man ten years my senior with a different job description than mine, I was moved by the way he carefully cared for and folded his clothes. His stack of khaki pants and white shirts looked a bit different than my seven piles of varying-sized T-shirts.

He smiled at me. I smiled back. And I relished the fact that, at the core, we are the same.

People operate from and share the same core human needs, which is actually where we must begin in order to genuinely engage in the Peace Project practices. When we connect at our shared core need, mercy's compassion invites us to "enter into the chaos of another"—because like laundry, everyone has it.

We are human. Unique in creation with intellect and the ability to reason. We are the only part of creation made in God's image, which uniquely, yet collectively, sets us apart. We alone in creation have an eternal aspect, a soul. That is a difficult concept to grasp. George MacDonald, writer and mentor to C. S. Lewis, put it this way: "You do not have a soul. You are a soul. You have a body." Matt Anderson, founder of Mere Orthodoxy, added his take on the famous quote: "You are a body. But you're a soul too. And your human flourishing is contingent upon being a soul-bodied thing."[2]

Maybe that's why thankfulness, kindness, and mercy—especially mercy—have such an impact. They engage us at a soul-level so the practicing of them offers opportunities to meet each other in our most raw and authentic selves. Mercy meets us in our chaos at our core, where core human needs to be loved, accepted, and known reside.

With my laundry finished and my heart full, almost as if I had experienced a "thin place" where the boundary between heaven and earth crumbles, I headed home. Upon arrival I was met with a barrage of questions. "What's for dinner?" "Where have you been?" "Did you remember to get me a Starbucks?" "How could you have left me?" Well, that last one was from our dog, Mitty. No words, just big, sad eyes full of betrayal at my going somewhere without him.

All these were followed by a question that was a bit more pressing. "What time do I need to be there tomorrow?"

Fury had the SAT coming up.

We have been around that block a few times before, and I have seen what a number attached to a score can do to my people. It tempts *soul-bodied things* to think that a score informs their worth or identity. I go to the mat on these things and fight for our kids' and their friends' thoughts—as it can be hard to believe the truth when faced with numbers that masquerade as life-definers.

The truth is Fury is not known by a number nor is his worth determined by a letter grade or team trophy or anything else. He is so much more than that. Never an object or a product, always a human being with an eternal aspect—more precious and treasured and loved than we can begin to imagine, loved with a kind of affection that is almost too much to receive.

In the world's economy, our identity is attained through achievement. But in God's economy, our identity has been determined and declared by him and our worth is received. According to him, we are masterpieces. And we get to walk life alongside each other—masterpieces in process.

And if we can see each other, as well as ourselves, as God sees us, then things change. Maybe it's times of suffering or challenge or places like the Laundromat that act as great equalizers and promote unity and help us to see a bit more clearly.

Not so long ago, bestselling author Sally Lloyd-Jones joined my friend Erin and me for a carpool chat. Carpool chats are yet another thing I have wrangled a few friends into doing with me. I thought inviting folks who know a lot more than I do to come and share their wisdom would be a great way to redeem the time sitting in a carpool line or sometimes at home in the kitchen. So, I started what I hope has been a fun and informative video podcast from the car, the *SaySomethingShow*.

People have been brave to join the ride that sometimes involves a fast-food drive-through for a Coke and some fries or other fun stops. Once our guest Janet Denison jumped my car battery gone dead as we got lost in conversation. Another time, seeing my tank on E, Johnny-on-the-spot author Max Lucado got to the pump before me to fill my empty tank on the way to the airport, where I had offered to drop him off as we chatted. We're excellent multitaskers.

I'm not sure Sally knew what she was getting into when she agreed to hop in the car on one of her trips to Dallas. But we became fast friends, and I still find myself lingering in the wisdom she offered.

One tidbit I just love (and have shared with a lot of folks) centered on a person's unique gifting and purpose and the freedom that comes with simply living it out. Over her life, Sally has watched what happens when others realize the beauty of people in the context of humanity as a whole.

"It's not about us," she said. "We're all part of this bigger more amazing story." She paused, then added, "When Londoners were asked—they'd lived through the Blitz—and many years later, people were asked, 'What was the happiest time of your life?' they all said, 'During the time of the Blitz,' which is completely mad. It was awful. People were getting bombed. And, when they were asked why, they said, 'Because we were pulling together. And we were part of a greater story.'"[3]

Maybe that's why mercy invites deep, soul-level freedom. Practicing mercy connects us to the greater story.

Maybe there's something about understanding people in the context of humanity and compassionately meeting someone in their chaos that takes us to that level playing field where we're all in it together—connecting and meeting each other at the soul-level. And it opens our eyes, even if only for a split second, so we can catch glimpses of goodness.

I thought about the *goodness* staring back at me as my cup filled with coffee that morning. And I even put the credit card back on top of the machine's start button. I wanted that sweet reminder of being known another time. I thought I might need it—not only for myself but as inspiration to offer such a reminder to someone else. Because even though days have been and can be hard and even though distracters and joy-sappers vie for our attention, the truth is—you and I are known. At the deepest level.

ALONGSIDE

TKM: Planting Seeds

I'm in the throes of parenting a teenager. And as I've participated in the Peace Project, I keep thinking back, wondering how I would have acted if my parents were trying to teach me about gratitude, kindness, and mercy. I'm sure I would have rolled my eyes just like my kid is doing to me.

What started as an exercise of teaching for the sake of teaching for me has become *doing* and *being* for the sake of planting seeds. Which I think will actually have a greater impact. It sure has had an impact on me.

I wish I had the things I'm learning from mercy when I was my daughter's age.

—NP—

TKM How have you practiced?
What have you learned?

Gratitude magnifies the spirit and promotes well-being. In good times and bad, authentic appreciation creates perspective, literally stepping back from the distractions of the moment and affirming something more lasting than passing circumstance.

ERIC MOSLEY AND DEREK IRVINE

DAY 6

Our Identity

> Sometimes your only available transportation is a leap of faith.
>
> MARGARET SHEPARD

Pulling into the parking lot, I reached for a receipt that I had taken extra care not to lose. I'm not the best at returning purchases we don't need. "I'll be right back," I told Snopes, who is always kind to ride along with me when she's in town from college.

I needed to return a rug I had purchased for Barton's dorm room. I knew it would be an easy stop. And I also knew that getting it done would make me feel good.

I walked into the store carrying the rug and stood waiting for the cashier to finish with another customer. Apparently I wasn't in the right spot, but I didn't know that at the time, so I stood patiently, waiting my turn. While I was standing there, a few folks started a different line across from me. So when I stepped up to the cashier, a lady raced toward me and blindsided me with rudeness. She literally hand-blocked me out of the way and told me to go to the back of the line.

It was so weird. Not only had I been standing there before anyone else but the few folks in the new line had seen me waiting my turn. It wasn't like I had come out of nowhere.

I looked around to see if I was being punked.

The cashier agreed with the lady. "For all purchases *or* returns, go there," she pursed-lip said, pointing me to the back of the now-formed line.

Stunned, I had no response. So what could I do but go to the back of the line?

On my way, I fought to find some kindness and mercy in my heart since I knew they can bring peace in the midst of a rude encounter. Honestly, I wanted to sass back and defend my customer line-rights (is that a thing?) *and* my place at the register because I was there before that lady. But instead, while fumbling my way to the back of the line, I halfheartedly muttered to myself, "Be nice—maybe she's a letter-of-the-law person, which can be a lot of pressure to live under, or maybe she has felt overlooked or something."

And a little mercy, along with kinder thoughts, made me feel better. Until the lady at the end of the line was rude to me too. She looked at me like I was coming at her with a cow prod instead of a 5x7 rug—that did not touch her. I was very careful. After turning her look of disgust away from me, she caught the eye of a different cashier who had been called to help with the new and now long line of customers. The lady shot the new cashier a nice head nod and eye roll at me for the two of them to share.

It was like I had a kick-me sign on my front.

The whole thing had me unsettled. I mean, what in the world? I was just trying to return a rug. Something good. Something responsible and productive. Doing that day what I could have, and usually do, put off until another day.

So I again searched to find mercy in my heart for the people around me. This woman must have been under a lot of stress because her response, though I *was* holding a clunky rug, did not seem warranted. Surely she was just in a sour mood, and I happened to be the one close by for her to unload some of her frustrations. I wanted to tell her that I saw the shared eye roll but knew that entering into someone's chaos with fists up would only end with both of us bloodied.

The feeling that I had a kick-me sign on my front instantly brought to mind a different sign. A name tag sort of sign. A proverbial name tag that, though unseen, was real and stays with me all the time. A name tag that does not read *kick me*, *punching bag*, *doormat*, *unseen*, or *insignificant*. No. If I'm going to be defined by anything, it's an eternal-truth name tag that reads *precious*, *sought after*, *beloved*—all reminders to me that I belong, am seen, and have worth. These descriptors are not according to me but are determined by God. And that's a game changer—a heart changer.

So as I stood with that big rug in my arms, I chose compassion, even though I didn't completely feel it. Extending mercy did not mean I was rolling over with an invitation to keep belittling me. But it was an act of sympathy, which came from a place of strength. Because I get it. I've had bad days and short fuses. I'm sure I've likely invited someone into an eye roll at another person's expense. And, even though I know that God has determined my identity, I forget.

In that moment, questions of mercy prompted my thoughts. *What if she doesn't know her great worth? What if she's worn down by trying to earn a name tag and doesn't know its gift has been purchased for her, paid for out of superlative love?*

About that time, mercy's compassion became real. Unsettled was replaced by settled. And I breathed easier. I was no longer caught in a need to prove or defend myself. Why should I allow minor inconvenience to steal peace or make me see the folks traveling alongside me as less than what they are—people of great worth, soul-bodied things?

Over the first few days of the Peace Project experiment, one aspect of purposefully practicing thankfulness, kindness, and mercy that consistently blew us away was the *immediate* peace that entered situations when we let these practices take over. We didn't ask for the peace; it just showed up and surprised us.

I think part of it comes from mercy's grounding. It's as if mercy shows us our eternal name tag every time it's tapped. Because mercy's compassion, grace, and forgiveness can only come from their source—God, who has determined our worth and our identity. These unspoken reminders of settled identity naturally ignite when we practice mercy. That's what ushers in peace and joy.

Identity and worth are interesting aspects of our being, our humanness, and they pop up in all sorts of places and ways. We let all sorts of things—ranging from grades to associations to origins to careers—form and inform our identity. Psychologist Janna Koretz reveals that we can take it further than we realize by sharing the story of Dan, a high-powered executive.

> Psychologists use the term "enmeshment" to describe a situation where the boundaries between people become blurred, and individual identities lose importance. Enmeshment prevents the development of a stable, independent sense of self. Dan, like many in high-pressure jobs, had become enmeshed not with another person, but with his career.[1]

Dan's problem was his career. We can fill in the blank for whatever walk in life we find ourselves. We focus our judgment on ourselves, then others, and back to ourselves as we become concerned with others' opinions of us. We enmesh our worth to identifiers.

I catch myself watching for such things in my kids, in myself, in people next to whom I walk through life. Are we functionally trusting accolades, achievements, events, and such to determine our worth and identity? If we really understood our worth, as determined by God rather than all the things that promise to make us okay, the volume on so many issues in and around our lives would be turned way down. Almost all of which hinge on our core human need to be seen and accepted.

Maybe it's these needs that prompted the cash register–line response in me. Not wanting to be overlooked or lose a place in line, though seemingly silly, may have had deeper roots. In psychological terms being acknowledged is a, if not *the*, core human need: the "need to be known and valued by self and by others."[2] It's woven in our sinews: this need to be both known and valued.

We can get stuck or sink into criticism when faced with the *self* aspect of the formula and easily fall at the mercy of *others*—a fairly fickle and highly unreliable prospect to which we can so easily hand off something as precious and tender as our worth.

Do we believe? Can we receive what God says about our identity and worth? Do we surrender our thoughts to the point of actually letting God's declaration define us from our inmost being to our outward self—even to the point where striving can cease?

As we practice thankfulness, kindness, and mercy, our identity plays a significant role, especially in being able to engage with mercy. In order to genuinely practice any of these virtues for extended periods of time, not as simple one-off actions, we must be willing to come from a settled place of strength. Not doing things in order to be liked or accepted but because our identity is informed by God rather than being subject to or linked to the value and acceptance of others or ourselves.

It might be hard to believe, especially during years when acceptance, belonging, and being known seem to endlessly dart just outside of our reach, but such love from the one who is love is worth considering. Because God considers us valuable.

In a beautiful example of this, US Senate Chaplain Barry Black shared a story about his mother at the 2017 National Prayer Breakfast. When he and his brother were kids, their mother would require them to memorize Bible verses. She would pay the boys a quarter for each verse they set to memory. Predictably, they would search the Bible to find and memorize the shortest verses in order to rack up their cash. Of course, their mother caught on. So she chose to put a few key verses in front of them, purposefully planting seeds so that they might know their worth.

One such passage was 1 Peter 1:18–19. "For you know that it was not with perishable things such as silver or gold that you were redeemed from the empty way of life handed down to you from your ancestors, but with the precious blood of Christ."

Upon memorizing and unavoidably thinking about these words, Black shared that even

> as a ten-year-old boy, [I] had enough analytical power to know that the value of an object is based upon the price someone is willing to pay. When it dawned on me—a little guy from the inner-city—that God sent what John 3 calls in the Greek the "*monogenes, the only one of its kind,"* the only begotten son, to die for me, no one was ever able to make me feel inferior again.[3]

Yes, the value of an object is based on what someone is willing to pay. And that payment is once and for all. Our being made right means we can be certain that we never have to feel inferior again. Even when we make ourselves feel inferior.

God gave everything because, to him, we are worth it. Dare we allow that to inform our worth and to inform the undeniable worth of the people walking next to us—today and every day?

It's almost too good to be true. Like a fairy tale.

Believing and embracing the superlative worth of a person (including the one in the mirror) is a lifelong journey paved by opportunities to practice and to encourage each other along the way.

So, while standing there in the line returning my rug, I was handed one of those opportunities. And I began at the good place to start—with thankfulness. Things I should be grateful for started popping into my thoughts, one after another, overpowering the words and attitudes slung my way by the folks in line. The rug in my arms prompted me to think of the kid who I thought would be using it. *I'm thankful for her in so many deep and meaningful ways. Thankful we could buy her a rug. Thankful for a store that welcomes returns.* And on it went.

Gratitude softened my heart. It prompted genuine compassion for the people around me. I don't know their story. They could have had a horrible day or who knows what. I felt compassion for the rude lady in front of me. She looked tired. I wondered what was going on in her life to make her crabby. And just at that moment, an opportunity to help her presented itself to me—which I did.

Rather than watch her dig through her bag, searching for change to complete her purchase under the watchful (and seemingly judgmental) eye of the cashier, I nabbed the chance to make up the difference on her cash payment. And she accepted my help. She kind of growled at me, but I didn't care.

My thoughts had been redirected. And peace quietly rolled in like a reliable ocean tide.

TKM How have you practiced?
What have you learned?

Sometimes your only available transportation is a leap of faith.

MARGARET SHEPARD

DAY 7

Mindsight Isn't 20/20

> The soul becomes dyed with the color of its thoughts.
>
> MARCUS AURELIUS

Yesterday, when dropping off the kids at school, these simple words crossed my lips, "Wow, we got here in great time." Because we had. Without speeding or a single quick stop.

But what I said and what a kid in the back seat heard were two very different things.

Fury's response to the simple statement: "IT'S NOT MY FAULT I COULDN'T FIND MY SHORTS!"

What?

"Wait." I stopped him before a waterfall of blames, excuses, and stress filled the car. "What did you hear me say?"

"You said that we were late because of me."

Welcome to what we call mindsight, a little something that involves seeing as well as hearing since it focuses on the way our minds perceive situations. Long before realizing *mindsight* was a neurobiological term coined by UCLA psychology professor

Dan Siegel, my family and I have used it (errantly, I'm sure) to describe unspoken yet very real communication. It comes in the form of loud conversations that play out in our thoughts and lay the groundwork for a lot of miscommunication.

Which is where things were heading in the car. What Fury heard really wasn't what I had said. And even though he likely perceived my attitude as frustrated as he watched me drive, I wasn't at all. (I made every light, which never happens!)

But I get it.

Also I had gone to the car while the boys were last-minute gathering their things, so I had no idea he had been frantically searching for shorts, not wanting to make anyone late.

"I didn't even know you were racing for the car," I assured him. "Let alone stressed about being late. I was just commenting about our luck in making every light."

"Oh."

His mind had told him a story that he bought hook, line, and sinker. Because that's the way his mind saw it. And usually our minds go negative.

It's not just an issue for kids.

We recently had a houseguest who thankfully knows us well enough to make herself at home. We love when people make themselves at home. It makes them family.

As the kids were grabbing breakfast and getting their stuff together, I noticed our friend was about to pour some cereal from the box in her hand. I quickly asked, "Was that box open?"

She looked at me, a little uncertain. "Yes?" Her eyes hinted that my question may have landed wrong.

Instead of letting her think up reasons I didn't want her to enjoy a fresh bowl of cereal, I jumped to explain my question. "No. It's okay!" I motioned for her to fill her bowl. "I was asking because Birdie saw a roach by the door yesterday. It was more of a water bug." (Side note: Ick! I have no love for the roach creature, especially those of the Godzilla variety that have been known to fly.)

"I would rather you open a *new* box of cereal than find a surprise inside." I don't think I could recover or ever eat cereal again if one of those ever made its way into a box from which I filled my bowl. Oh, the thought of it!

She laughed and almost audibly sighed.

No stranger to Texas, this friend had seen many a ginormous bug in her day. "Gosh, when you asked, I thought you meant for me to eat from an open box instead of opening a new box." I could tell it was more than that. My comment, intended for good, had landed heavy. Instead of feeling cared for, she felt a sting. As if I were implying that she wasn't worth a new box but only the dregs of an old, stale box, which couldn't be further from the truth. It was just mindsight.

Rarely is mindsight 20/20; it's usually negative.

Kendra Cherry, author and educational specialist, refers to this knee-jerk mental reaction as *negative bias*, our human "tendency not only to register negative stimuli more readily but also to dwell on these events." And "this bias toward the negative leads [us] to pay much more attention to the bad things that happen, making them seem much more important than they really are."

She continues:

> We tend to learn more from negative outcomes and experiences. We even tend to make decisions based on negative information more than positive data. It is the "bad things" that grab our attention, stick to our memories, and, in many cases, influence the decisions that we make.[1]

We are quick to hear and receive the negative, needing at least five positive comments to outweigh one negative. Even when the comments or conversations occur silently in our thoughts.

That morning in the car, Fury was carrying a heavy load of messaging that couldn't have been further from the truth. But after we outed the negativity and laughed about how we all tend to overhear (as in hearing more than is said), a delightful new door opened for he and his siblings to start a game of what-Mom-says versus what-*we*-hear. Fun times in the car.

What Mom says: "Have you finished your homework?"
What we hear: "You fail everything! Why can't you be smart like your sister?"

What Mom says: "Why don't you wear that cute new dress we bought?"
What we hear: "You look fat in what you have on."

What Mom says: "Did you remember to brush your teeth?"
What we hear: "Your breath smells like poop."

What Mom says: "You should call Katie to go on a run with you."
What we hear: "You ARE fat."

What Mom says: "It must be hot outside."
What we hear: "You reek. Go take a shower."

That last one is probably true.

No wonder they think there's more behind my words—which is usually not the case, mostly because I could never keep up with it all. I'm sure my siblings and I did the same with our mom. We probably still do. Siblings, couples, children, students—all of us read into what we hear. Everyone (everyone!) has stepped foot in the not-hearing-what-is-actually-being-said minefield and will do so again.

Author Lysa TerKeurst shared a little about our natural bent toward mental storytelling on one of our *SaySomething* chats. She told us about a lovely junior high experience where not only was everyone invited to a party—except for her—but they had matching pink T-shirts that they wore to school and in the carpool that took them to the party:

> We all have a story. And we all have a story we tell ourselves.
>
> So the story that day was: She probably just didn't even think I was close enough friends with her to invite me to the birthday party. End of story.
>
> But the story I was telling myself is: I'm never going to be good enough. Like, I'm always going to have to navigate this feeling of being slightly left out, slightly forgotten, or being completely overlooked.[2]

Lysa then brought in today's terms with social media and all that can fake-remind us of our junior high insecurities and the inevitable questioning, doubting, and judgment we sometimes feel. "Why in the world do I keep asking myself, 'Am I good enough?'" Which she followed up with an answer: "Because God never intended me to just be good enough. God intended me to be better than that."[3]

Our thoughts are worth noticing, calling out, and fighting for.

Because what occupies our thoughts *greatly* impacts our peace, our contentment, our soul-health, and our actions. American philosopher Dallas Willard offers this insight.

> Now we need to understand that what simply occupies our mind very largely governs what we do.
>
> It sets the emotional tone out of which our actions flow, and it projects the possible courses of action available to us. Also the mind, though of little power on its own, is the place of our widest and most basic freedom. . . .
>
> Of all the things we do, we have more freedom with respect to what we will think of, where we will place our mind, than anything else.[4]

Which is pretty exciting. It reminds me of Chuck Swindoll's quote, "Life is 10 percent what happens to me, 90 percent how I react to it."[5] We don't get to choose what happens to us, but we do get to choose our attitude. Rather than take the bait and hand our thoughts or emotions over to fear, frustration, or anger (even when warranted)—we can breathe. We can grab hold of perspective instead of surrendering our thoughts or perceptions to mindsight. Then, maybe we can come at whatever is hitting us from a foundation grounded in safety, provision, acceptance, and love—from God, rather than ever-shifting foundations.

Sometimes, in order to do so, we have to be willing to be honest and aware. This is where coming alongside each other can be most helpful. At the core, there is nothing new under the sun or unique to any of us. Couldn't we all relate to Lysa's *good enough* or my son's carpool miscommunication or even our houseguest whose thoughts instantly traveled to insignificance rather than worth?

For all of us, it can be hard to recognize, let alone call out, thoughts that have gone rogue. The key is that we're not alone, as in: we can help each other. Fresh eyes see more clearly. And honest assessments, though possibly painful in the moment, invite freedom. The more we call out mindsight mishaps together, the easier it gets to do it ourselves. Plus, strength lies in numbers. And we never need to walk alone. Wonky mindsight multiplies when we isolate ourselves. The hard part is parking our stubborn ways long enough to get help from others.

Slowing down, breathing, and taking things a bit less personally offers freedom from frustration and freedom to respond with reason—even if the response is to ourselves, simply to settle our thoughts. Together we can grab some perspective lenses that just might give our thoughts a break, which might allow us to give others a break as well.

TKM How have you practiced?
What have you learned?

The soul becomes dyed with the color of its thoughts.

MARCUS AURELIUS

DAY 8

Thankfulness Takes On Fear

> When a resolute young fellow steps up to the great bully, the world, and takes him boldly by the beard, he is often surprised to find it comes off in his hand, and that it was only tied on to scare away the timid adventurers.
>
> RALPH WALDO EMERSON

Yesterday I went to the movies with my two oldest kids.

Shocker of all shockers—we were early! That means we got to see the trailers. All was fun and fine until my daughter turned to me and said, "Don't watch this!"

Hilarious that she was telling me to avert my eyes. The tables sure have turned. Does that mean I'm old? Best not to answer.

"This is a trailer for the new *It*," she loud-whispered.

I guess there's a take 2 for that gem. And though I never saw the first one (scary movies and I have never been friends), I know I don't want to. I looked over at my young adult kids and both of them had their ears plugged and eyes down. So I followed their lead and did the same. At the creepy music climactic end of the trailer, we looked up. What could we do but laugh?

Which we did. Hilariously.

So we might have looked silly—but seriously, who wants to willingly invite fear into their lives? Especially that late-night kind that leads your thoughts into eerie places where clowns hide and pop up in the mirror behind you.

Because it's usually at night, in the dark, that fears rise.

Case in point, Birdie, our youngest, recently wandered into our room around midnight and poked me awake. I don't know if it was the storm barreling through Dallas or something he had seen that grabbed his thoughts, but there he stood. "Mom—I can't sleep."

And to me, one of life's greatest delights is the role of a parent to reassure and comfort. I rarely get to do it these days as the kids get older, but I relish the opportunity. Maybe because I get to hear the reassurances too—as they pass my lips.

"Everything is okay," I told him.

And together, since it can be so hard in the moment to redirect our thoughts, we put his late-night fears into perspective.

What is it with fear?

In certain forms, it almost instantly hijacks and takes the reins of our thoughts. Unlike the freedom that comes with thoughts and actions of gratitude, kindness, or mercy, anxious fear plants and almost cements thoughts directly onto ourselves—prompting everything but peace. Calling out misgivings like those that come with fear helps us deal with our own chaos so that mercy can do its magic.

It seems to me that there are three types of fear that cross our paths: two that alarm and one that steadies.

> Instinctive fear: fight-or-flight fear is sewn into the fabric of our body and triggers alarm for a reason (often for protection)
>
> Human-centric fear: fear that is informed by the world; usually fueled by doubt, pressures, stress, expectations,

> and the like, prompting alarm that can instantly overwhelm, then linger for good measure
>
> God-centric fear: not afraid of but awe and respect for; holy fear steadies us through trust in God, offering solid ground and calm-in-the-storm safety

Most fear involves and relies on things that are not seen. It tends to live in our minds and our thoughts, where we have already outed that mindsight is not 20/20.

We can't see or touch the source of our anxieties or worries, but they feel real, especially if we allow them to fester. Which is one of the reasons we need to be careful to take tender care of what goes in our minds. Because fear has a sneaky way of sparking other things. And once ignited, it finds life in an almost natural transfer of trust: we believe the fear and act. Which in the case of instinctive fear can save our lives, but in the case of human-centric fear can take us on a wild ride.

Fear undeniably intersects with faith: the assuredness of what is not seen. Faith invites action. And what we choose to do and how we act reveals the source of our functional trust. So in what are we trusting? Human-centric fear, anxiety, worry, and reasoning? Or God-centric fear, awe and respect—trusting in his all-powerful protection, provision, and love?

On a walk one morning, I chatted with a friend who was struggling with current fears, calling out what-if woes and calling down judgment upon folks for not "doing it right." Times involving change, unrest, and health scares like the COVID-19 pandemic invite fear, which is understandable. News cycles, conversations, and thoughts tend to be consumed with loads of what-ifs and finger-pointing. But, with mercy's compassion, we have the chance to help each other give equal airtime to gratitude. Which we did by literally calling out specific things in the same landscape for which to be grateful. She dialed down unsettledness related to the folks not "doing it right," of which I'm sure I have been one. And as perspective joined the conversation, we walked away breathing a bit easier, as what-if fears and uneasiness settled into a healthier balance.

Our thankfulness, kindness, and mercy practices play a role in getting perspective aligned to truth and putting things like fear, anxiety, and worry in their place. Reaching for truth and resting in God's provision, timing, sovereignty, and safety redirects fear to solid ground. Even in hard circumstances where fears gain ground.

We've definitely faced suffering around our house. And we have lobbed the question of how God and hurt go together when he's supposed to be good. I was blasted with that question at another movie theater, of all places, when Birdie was hit squarely with suffering and evil and the absolutely legitimate question—why? His childlike faith bumped up against some mature life topics. And it unsettled him.

This time it wasn't a trailer. It was the movie we chose to see as a family. The kids love history, so we decided to see the latest WWII film. I didn't realize, though I should have, the extent to which atrocities would play a part. Feel free to judge. I certainly judged myself. It was a family outing based on a recommendation from friends who took their same-aged child. But still. The sick feeling in my stomach comes back even thinking about it.

I sat next to Birdie and was ready to bolt not far into the film. There was a story line involving a pilot whose plane crashes in the English Channel. The thought of young soldiers drowning or lost at sea was too much. We didn't stick around long enough to see what happened next. The movie's good things were amazingly great—but the hardships were far from sugarcoated. Not long after the painful scenes flitted across the screen, I looked over at Birdie and said, "I'm ready to leave, are you?"

"Yes." He almost shuddered.

I grabbed his hand and we quickly exited, motioning to the others that we would meet up with them after the film's conclusion. His breathing quickened. He was clearly disturbed.

"Sweetheart . . . ," I began.

"Why would you take me to see a movie like that?!" he asked. My heart sank.

Why? I wondered too. *Why did we?* It seemed like a good idea at the time. I had no clue how it would so deeply disturb him. Maybe I should have known but sometimes you just don't.

We went outside and sat on a bench to wait for the movie to end.

"Why would God allow all that? War? The suffering? The death?" he asked. Then, in a whispered voice, he added, "The evil?" He shook his head, tears silently rolling down his cheeks.

"I'm so sorry you saw that," I said. "So sorry."

"I just don't understand." He was grappling to connect the God he knew as loving and kind, all-powerful and fully able to stop bad things with the cruel and tragic scenes he had watched on the movie screen.

I took a deep breath and started to do my best to explain something I can't begin to fully understand myself. But since we had already waded into these challenging waters by seeing the first half of the movie, they had to be crossed rather than avoided.

"I don't know. But I do know God is good," I said. "And I know God loves those people, like he loves us. And he allows evil to exist, which I think is somehow *for* us. That sounds weird." It does sound weird, and ridiculous, like trying to make Cinderella's shoe fit on another person's foot. But what I am sure of is that God is for us. Because he says it, not me.

"There is something in God allowing the dark to exist," I continued, "that opens the door to our being able to know him in light of faith—where we don't get to see it all, but we can choose to trust. Evil doesn't get to freely roam and do anything, anytime. Everything answers to God."

That is where I sat with Birdie, trying to get a clearer grasp on the mysteries of God, motivated to at least try to navigate the unavoidable topic since we had opened the door. I watched his mind whirling, searching for a place where his thoughts could land.

It's so hard for us to see it. And since light shines brightest in the dark, maybe that's part of the dark's purpose—to help us better see the good.

We talked about what Sally Lloyd-Jones had said about the Blitz, which occurred in the same time frame as the movie. About how she said that people actually considered that horrific period "the happiest time" of their lives because they came together, walking alongside rather than against each other. Birdie and I talked about the fact that hope is always at hand if he ever found himself in such dire straits. And it gave him hope for the boys in the film who historically did.

"From where we're standing," I offered Birdie, "suffering looks bad. But from God's point of view, maybe it looks like love."

I finished falling over my words and felt pretty inadequate, knowing that last comment opened a whole new set of questions. I looked down at Birdie.

"Okay," he said matter-of-factly, no longer visibly disturbed or shaken.

"What?" I asked, a bit floored that he had moved from fear and disappointment to peace.

"Okay," he said again. And he left it there. Not needing to know all the details but knowing that if God was in them—he was good to go.

I learn a lot from that kid.

Later he would tell me that he really wanted to stop crying more than anything. He didn't want people to see. He said he willed his tears to stop by thinking about things that were happening in the moment rather than the things of the past. How? Since practicing thankfulness was fresh in his mind, he went to gratitude. Apparently, he started ticking through things for which to be thankful. And that helped him get perspective. And it gave him time to breathe. He was able to find solid ground in reality rather than what he was seeing on a screen. The reality of today's day, not the reality of WWII days.

It's amazing to me that Birdie reached for gratitude to get unstuck.

And it worked. One thing about kids: they aren't faking it.

I'm thankful for kids walking alongside me who confidently, without a care in the world about what someone might think, can cry or cover their eyes and extend kindness by whisper-yelling at me to do the same. And I just love that they are willing to give themselves a break instead of forcing themselves to be okay with things that aren't okay. Even when the people sitting around them make a point to roll their eyes.

ALONGSIDE

THANKFULNESS: Fear Eradicator

I've started to realize that thankfulness even takes away fear.

For instance, when one of my kids started driving, all kinds of things that could go wrong started running through my head. But I really love the Brené Brown quote: "It's not possible to be stressed about something when you're being grateful for it." I can't stop thinking about it.

So, for driving, I put gratitude in the places that I knew my fear would creep into. I was thankful that my son is a good driver and has been well-trained. Which is where my worry would be—that he might not know what he's doing. I'm genuinely grateful for quality training—he really had a great teacher. I think about those things, and lo and behold the fear has taken a back seat.

I'm continually floored at the power of thankfulness—which is, for me, the easiest of the three. I can always find something to be thankful for. And it works! I even went to sleep the night he got his license—*before* he got home!

—BS—

TKM How have you practiced?
What have you learned?

When a resolute young fellow steps up to the great bully, the world, and takes him boldly by the beard, he is often surprised to find it comes off in his hand, and that it was only tied on to scare away the timid adventurers.

RALPH WALDO EMERSON

DAY 9

Settling Unsettled

> There are always flowers for those who want to see them.
>
> HENRI MATISSE

A couple of years ago, Birdie and I had a conversation that I find myself revisiting often. In the profound way he approaches life, he said something to me that has really stuck. He said it when we were doing what we do, driving. "Do you know why we can't see tomorrow?" he had looked over at me and asked.

"Why?" I asked back.

"Because we can only live today."

I've thought about it so many times since, because, yes, today is the day we get to live. And it's a fine day, even with all its goings-on, whether good or bad. Today is the only day we get, so why not live it rather than try to relive yesterday or let tomorrow's expectations, worries, stresses, or even hopes steal from it?

Our thoughts are so prone to wander. And as we've already outed, they go negative fast. Which is where we have already witnessed, even after only a few short days, the power of practicing gratitude, kindness, and mercy.

Snopes and I talked about living today's day as she joined our dog, Mitty, and me for a walk. I was thankful she did, as she had been recently staring down some unknowns. A walk always seems to help order thoughts, so as we made our way around the block, I asked her how she felt.

"Unsettled," she answered.

In a conversation earlier in the day, a friend of mine had used the same word, as she, too, had a plate scattered with uncertainty. Lots of moving parts. Lots of complicated family circumstances that she would have never imagined a few years ago.

Unsettled. What a good word. So honest and on point. I loved the openness of both my friend and my daughter.

I think that such matter-of-fact responses are one of suffering's silver linings. Feelings that accompany challenging days are easily called out because they're so close to the surface. In times of hardship, pressures to maintain appearances or to put on a good face are much more easily back-burnered as none of that matters.

Hardship or not, Pollyanna responses aren't what's important: people are. And every person bumps into unsettled now and then. So, rather than let *unsettled* have a heyday with our thoughts, we can grab a lifeline. Together we can call out specifics and reach for *settled.*

Settled looks like acknowledging the hardship with all its what-ifs. Settled is encouraging each other to live what is happening now, not what might be. Settled reaches for reason and perspective—reminding each other that people are resilient and tenacious with loads of history to prove it. Settled anchors thoughts in the provision for today. Settled is trust. Settled is alongside—not alone.

Because life is complicated, especially when we calculate all the chaos we each bring to the table. But in the midst of unsettled and complicated, true treasure can be found. Practicing thankfulness, kindness, and mercy brings the treasure out from the shadows and into the spotlight so it is easy to see, even on days we don't feel like looking.

Silver linings help us

> see life as a journey, not a moment
> hang on to the beautiful revelation that people matter
> embrace freedom
> experience provision—manna provision, daily sustenance that is absolute and sufficient
> rest in grace that is not contingent on performance

How can peace flourish in moments that feel anything but peaceful? I don't know, but I know it can. Which is what I think has been one of the more significant aspects of the Peace Project so far. The refocus of gratitude alongside the action point of kindness, added to the soul-adjustment of mercy, invites peace and hope and ditch despair.

I can't help but wonder if practicing thankfulness removes cataracts in our soul-sight, revealing depth perception and taking black and white to Technicolor. Thankfulness brings into focus the greater story. Is it thankfulness that breaks apart life's burdens? Is practicing thankfulness a torch that lights our way? It certainly lightens the load.

So for today I'm thankful for all the silver linings available to us upon our journey. Thankful for the people walking alongside—my friends and my kids who are willing to play when I come up with weird ideas.

Because life is complicated.

Today, in the midst of mad dashes, we can practice kindness by dropping off a fresh-cut flower arrangement to a neighbor recently affected by a sadness. We all have someone in our lives, or maybe even someone standing by us in a line, who is experiencing hardships and could use an encouraging word, deed, or some alongside-grieving.

Encouraging words show up in all sorts of places and ways. It was during the walk with Mitty that Snopes honestly outed feeling unsettled. And, as if on cue, we came across some chalk musings from our friendly neighborhood sidewalk prophet. This neighbor leaves messages of encouragement on her front walk for all the passersby and pups to see.

On this day, she had written:

> It's not happiness that brings us gratitude.
> It's gratitude that brings us happiness.

Well, that's one way to snuff unsettled.

A neighborly reminder to be thankful for all we have and are, rather than be overwhelmed by unsettled, made us both smile. None of us are on this journey alone. We're walking alongside each other as regular people, each of whom, though living through different circumstances, can be encouraged by the same words of truth.

This Peace Project has been an adventure. Each of us has loved seeing and sometimes being surprised by what is in store to learn each day—in a strangely safe and exciting way—even on unsettled days that don't look like or go the way we thought they would.

ALONGSIDE

GRATITUDE: And the Mundane

I have really loved considering the idea that every breath we draw is a gift of God's love—it's something that has hit me on this Peace Project experiment.

We take so much for granted, even simple activities like leaving and coming home. It's something we do every day—and it just seems mundane. But doing the mundane *with gratitude* has so deeply touched me.

The idea of being grateful for every breath has powerfully impacted me.

—SJ—

TKM How have you practiced?
What have you learned?

There are always flowers for those who want to see them.

HENRI MATISSE

DAY 10

Mercy's Compassion

> Our human compassion binds us the one to the other—not in pity or patronizingly, but as human beings who have learnt how to turn our common suffering into hope for the future.
>
> NELSON MANDELA

Can kindness change a life?

According to Leon Logothetis, author, producer, and host of the popular Netflix series *The Kindness Diaries*, the answer is yes.

I agree. Not only can kindness affect life change but it's almost always a positive change. Practicing kindness prompts a view shift and invites action, which takes thoughts and makes them an experience, going the extra mile toward new neuropathways of peace.

Like an optometrist adjusting a prescription (*better now? or now?*), kindness exchanges lenses so that the viewer can see more clearly. But unlike prescription lenses that simply sharpen vision, kindness works toward a complete view shift. It takes our eyes off of ourselves. Not just ourselves but off all things *us*: self-preservation, self-promotion, self-hate, self-deprecation . . . fill in the blank. And a view shift plants our eyes on others, not through comparison but compassion that opens a door to mercy.

In the process of a view shift, we get to see people traveling alongside instead of in opposition to us; we see the unseen. And we see people not as products or objects but as soul-inhabited humans.

Kindness is powerful that way. And kindness is contagious. It's harder to receive than to dish out, yet receiving kindness is almost as important as giving it.

When Leon came to Dallas a few years ago, he kindly braved our carpool chat to share about his adventures around the world that were fueled solely by the kindness of strangers.[1] Leon set out with nothing more than a yellow motorcycle that he named Kindness 1, some clothes, and complete reliance on the kindness of strangers. No cash. No plans. Just hope and an expectation that kindness would prevail.

"Of all the people that you met along the way," I asked him, "who would you say stuck on you more than any other? If that's fair?" I didn't want to put one person's help over another's—especially with such a humble, others-centered subject.

He was quick to respond. "Tony. Tony was the homeless chap."

Tony, who lived in Pittsburgh, saw Leon's need and stepped up. Tony gave from absolutely nothing. He had so little, yet he shared his food, his makeshift shelter, and his time. In fact, Tony was quick to extend kindness when others wouldn't.

"When Tony discovered my predicament," Leon told us, "his response was simple. 'I don't have a home,' he told me, 'but you can stay with me.'" Tony let Leon into his world for the day and made a pallet for him to stay the night in his makeshift home. Leon has since said that one night with Tony changed his life forever because his kindness showed Leon that "true wealth is in our hearts not in our wallets."

So much of what transpired is amazing. In receiving kindness from Tony (who had almost nothing), Leon gave dignity to someone resigned to being unseen. "In that moment, we both saw each other," Leon marveled.

What a beautiful thing. That view shift spoke to both men at the core of their beings. Their souls collided through acts set apart for us as humans: seeing and loving others, sharing, giving, and calling each other by name are all acts fueled by kindness and mercy's compassion. Tony intimately knew what it feels like to be unseen, unheard, and rejected. Through compassionate lenses, he saw Leon and stepped up bravely to offer what little he had.

All of us in the carpool chat were lifted by Leon's stories. Even Leon seemed moved as he recounted them. We lingered in the goodness of it all. Then Courtney asked, "Is something woven throughout the globe that is the same no matter where, no matter what?"

"Yes," Leon again responded instantly, yet thoughtfully. "In every country, everyone—irrespective of wealth, irrespective of age, irrespective of color, irrespective of religion—just wants to be seen, just wants to be valued, just wants to feel like they matter."

A universal truth.

Kindness—we need to give it and we need to be able to receive it. Maybe that's why it has the power to change a life.

Before our carpool chat ended, Leon left us with something wonderful. "Love is seeing someone."

Compassion and sympathetic consciousness allow us to take another's perspective and lessen our propensity to objectify others by how they might benefit us. Compassion is useless if taken too far, to the detriment of ourselves. We can easily overfeel by taking on someone's burden, which incapacitates us and makes it impossible for us to walk alongside them.

I like the term *compassionomics,* coined by the physician/scientist team Stephen Trzeciak and Anthony Mazzarelli. Compassionomics provides overwhelming evidence for the healing power of compassion. As physicians, Trzeciak and Mazzarelli focused on the compassion needed to handle patients in the medical profession. And they discovered that compassion, like gratitude and kindness—however accessed and put into motion—affects our brains in positive ways.

> There is neuroscience research using MRI scans to support this. When a person experiences empathy, the pain centers in the brain are activated. But when a person is focused on compassion—the action component of trying to alleviate another's suffering—a different area of the brain, a "reward" pathway, is activated.[2]

Opportunities to practice compassion abound. Mercy's compassion is the fuel to practicing kindness, the physical action of doing something for others. We see it in examples like Tony and Leon.

I recently had the opportunity to reach for compassion as I stumbled my way down the stairs to get a cup of coffee early in the morning. A lovely menagerie of junk all over our kitchen island greeted me. Snopes and I had gotten home late the night before from a trip to San Antonio to visit Barton, so I didn't see the piles until the early hours of the next day. The boys had done their best to hold down the fort while the girls traveled, but apparently had lost sight of the kitchen.

I looked at the clutter and wondered why. Why the multiple open cereal boxes? Why so many? Why not just close them and put them away? And why dirty clothes on the kitchen counter? Why leave out an empty carton of milk? I didn't understand and felt a tiny twinge of *Really?* begin to rise. But I stopped it midthought. And I reached for gratitude for all they had done while we were gone (including a certain son who not only loaded the dishwasher but started it too!). Once I experienced that view shift, I happily tidied up. Compassion put the cleaning into motion. Rather than making it about me and what I had to do, I focused instead on all they had done, even though they had full plates. Thankfulness, kindness, and mercy were at play, making it a breeze to finish the kitchen and easy to start the laundry without resentment or indignation. The boys had put things in the washer; they just forgot to hit start. The story of my life. Apparently the easily distracted apples don't fall far from the tree.

So that was at 6:30 a.m.

Fast-forward to 11:30 a.m. and (BAM!) another opportunity for kindness and mercy arrived as a minivan-mom turned in front of me, making sure I didn't pull ahead of her. She stared me down and honked for good measure. She even paused to catch my eye as she waved a certain finger emphatically at me, taking her time to be sure I understood her disdain.

I turned to Snopes and sighed. "Well, I'm not feeling it, but here's our mercy opportunity. Something stressful and hard must be going on in her life to prompt all that. Maybe something with one of those kids." She had a stick-figure-family decal on her back window.

In that moment I was still trying to find a place to put all she dished our way. But saying the word *mercy* out loud made me genuinely feel for her and wish I had been quicker to practice kindness—quicker to find compassion and possibly say a kind word in my heart instead of grumbling. There were a lot of stick figure decals on that back window, an indication of her own full plate. My compassion was sincere.

Arriving home, I had the opportunity to be merciful to myself, which is strangely the hardest.

In all the hubbub of the day, I threw away a receipt—a big one. And, in my morning kitchen counter declutter, I tossed what I had put aside to save. This prompted some dumpster diving. In the heat of the day. After I had already showered—yes, this is our life.

I was SO grateful the trash guys had not picked anything up yet because I found it! Then I walked back in the house hot, tired, thirsty—and a little sad as I spied some of Barton's things. Because I miss the kids when they're gone.

But on my now-clean counter sat a bottle of water from the weekend trip, and my thoughts were flooded with things for which to be grateful—like that beautiful bottle of water that our lovely hotel (where we scored a great rate) had generously put in our room. I was grateful for the nice friends Barton has made at school, for safe travel, for sisters who love each other—gosh, the list could go on and on. And what seemed like an uphill challenge in the moment instantly turned into smooth gliding as gratitude's gravity took over.

I grabbed Mitty and headed out for a walk.

The minute I opened the door, I glimpsed something that gave me a blast of oxygen-enriched perspective: the setting sun. Experiencing a sunrise or sunset almost always reframes life. Looking up broadens our horizon and literally prompts deep breathing. Looking up offers wide views and allows us to see beyond a moment and welcome the bigger picture.

Here's the thing we're learning about practicing thankfulness, kindness, and mercy—the more we use them, the more they appear without need of an invitation. It's almost reflex.

And what a great side effect: a thankfulness/kindness/mercy reflex.

ALONGSIDE

MERCY: A Power Move

Before doing this experiment, I'm not sure I'd ever thought about mercy. But I am now.

This weekend, one of my kids was dragging his feet and made us late. Typically, I would have threatened *this* and yelled *that* and, quite frankly, been unkind.

But with Soul30 on my mind, I gave him grace. And we didn't spend our drive mad because I didn't go to all that ugliness thanks to mercy.

Having mercy's compassion on my mind made it easy to recall the heavy things that were going on in his life and saved us a lot of conflict. I'm grateful.

—LP—

TKM How have you practiced?
What have you learned?

Our human compassion binds us the one to the other—not in pity or patronizingly, but as human beings who have learnt how to turn our common suffering into hope for the future.

NELSON MANDELA

DAY 11

Mercy's Forgiveness

> Forgiveness is not an occasional act, it is a constant attitude.
>
> MARTIN LUTHER KING JR.

Birdie recently asked me about forgiveness.

"Did you hear that song?" he asked. He was talking about a song on the radio that compared the vastness of forgiveness to the ocean. Then he said, "Pretty ridiculous. Apparently, you'd have to know how many drops are in the ocean to be able to know how many times you can be forgiven."

I looked over at him. He was going literal on me—something these boys so often do. "I think it's saying that God's forgiveness is immeasurable." We'll never know how many times to ask for forgiveness or to forgive. Sometimes we don't even realize when we need it. Which is the point. You're forgiven. All of it.

He thought for a minute and asked the next logical question, "So then why ask for it?"

This kid. The deep things he contemplates, even in the morning on the way to school, are always fun to discuss. He could use a seasoned theologian or philosopher in the carpool. But I'm what he's got.

"I think the asking is for us," I offered. "So we're aware of our need for forgiveness. Then maybe we can change and be free from it."

Awareness is one of the paths to change, and change can lead to freedom—freedom from mitigating wrong actions that we try to justify. Or maybe it's freedom from blame. Since blame invites judgment and keeps our eyes anchored on us. The freedom thing is huge. And so are the compassion and empathy that come with it—since we've all been there.

"Like when y'all told me to stop playing on the iPad yesterday," Birdie offered as an example. We were watching church online and had asked him to put the screen down. He heard, but didn't listen and kept playing, erroneously assuming that we couldn't see him as he tried to hide it under a blanket.

He's so cute. I love how he runs toward honest discourse. "Oh, that." I nodded. "It did take you a while to admit it." We had caught him in the act but still made him admit what he had done. It took a bit for him to come around, though he finally did.

He sheepishly grinned.

"Why didn't you want to let go of it?" I asked him.

"I didn't think it was fair that you and Dad asked me to stop. My way seemed right, so I chose it over yours."

So candid. "But how did that make you feel?"

"Honestly?" He looked over at me. "It felt good."

"Seriously?"

"Yes, I didn't think about the lying part." Then he looked straight at me and tease-grimaced. "Until you asked *and* spelled it out. *Then* I realized that I really had done something wrong. The whole thing was so frustrating."

"So how did you feel coming clean?"

"Better." I could see his thoughts running through the entire scenario—even the subsequent punishment: sweeping, raking, and picking up some of the gazillion acorns that never stop dropping in our yard. His slow-motion sweeping and bagging effort was on display for all of us to see. But so was his dad, who quietly went outside to join the sweeping without a word.

"Yes. Better," he said again. "I hate to say it, because you'll probably remind me, but I think admitting helped me get over it."

It is weird but real. Admitting is the first step toward freedom, even when there are consequences.

"I think that's how forgiveness from God must be," he continued. "Yep, forgiveness that is so big, it's . . . like drops in the ocean." Birdie nodded. "That makes more sense now."

Forgiveness. It's vast not only in its width but clearly also in its depth. The power of it is undeniable, especially as it permeates even the most challenging circumstances, far more serious than an iPad fib, and leads to mercy.

Not long ago we, along with the rest of the world, had a front-row seat to watch forgiveness in action play out in a Dallas courtroom. Amber Guyger, a former Dallas police officer, was convicted of killing a man named Botham Jean in an unusual circumstance. Unaware she was on the wrong floor, Guyger entered Jean's apartment thinking it was hers. Falsely assuming him to be an intruder, she pulled out her gun. The scenario turned tragic fast, leaving a family's makeup forever altered and a young woman's life trajectory permanently changed.

During the sentencing portion of Guyger's murder trial, Jean's family had an opportunity to speak their piece. The surprise came when Botham's brother, Brandt, presented Guyger with a speech not of hatred but of love. Before he finished speaking, he looked at her and said, "I forgive you." He even went so far as to ask the judge permission to give Guyger a hug. Amid gasps and disbelief in the courtroom, he did. And between deep sobs, she melted into his shoulder.

The power of forgiveness spoke volumes—drowning out the noise of the protestors outside the courtroom who were shouting their rage at the incident's societal aspects. Brandt's act of forgiveness was the lead story on every major network. It spread across the airwaves and around the world, heralding thoughts of healing rather than rage and anger.[1]

Similarly, after the Charleston, South Carolina, church shooting in 2015, the power of forgiveness stood ready to do what it does: usher in life. *USA Today* reported that "in a world where evil can seem unstoppable, these families from Charleston have demonstrated that there is still hope. Hope not only in the good fight against racism, prejudice and evil, but hope also in the good that overwhelms evil . . . via counterintuitive forces: compassion, mercy and forgiveness."[2]

June Hunt, author, speaker, and founder of Hope for the Heart ministry, offered her insight based on years of counseling listeners on her syndicated radio program, as well as what she learned from forgiving her own father.

> After becoming a Christian, I had been learning about the love, mercy, and forgiveness of God . . . yet, I still felt justified in holding on to my hatred. Forgiving my father seemed wrong, primarily because he had not changed. I especially couldn't grasp my mother's kindness toward him. To be candid, at times my mother's kindness felt wrong—even offensive. I thought: Someone needs to let him know how wrong he is!
>
> . . . Finally, I realized, I needed to take the burden of not forgiving my father off my "emotional hook" and put him on God's "hook." The Lord says . . . "It is mine to avenge" (Deuteronomy 32:35).[3]

Forgiveness doesn't mean saying that what someone has done is right or asking that victims submit to further mistreatment. Forgiveness is letting go, not condoning what happened.

Dr. Tony Evans, pastor and bestselling author, put it another way.

> Many of us today find ourselves on a leash. The links in the chain are anger, bitterness, resentment, and revenge. All these, however, come down to one thing—unforgiveness. Unforgiveness holds us hostage, and when we try to pull away, it pulls us right back and we find ourselves prisoners of what someone else has done to us or perhaps what we have done to ourselves.[4]

Evans has also said that "unilateral forgiveness means I forgive so that I can move on. I forgive so that I can let go. I forgive so that I can go get the dent fixed."[5]

Forgiveness and grace act as the sparks that set mercy's embers aflame. And as is often the case, it blesses the giver as much, if not more, than the one on the receiving end.

Still in our car, we were waved into our lane by the carpool monitor. Birdie and I were lingering, chewing on our forgiveness conversation.

I for one was overwhelmed. Not with usual things, like all I needed to get done. Not with the tests that were on the other side of the car door that would absolutely beg to inform the self-worth of the kid about to take them. Not with my throat that was starting to hurt or the dread of possibly getting the flu that had been running through our house. Not at the news I had listened to that morning that seemed filled with discord, blamings, bombings, and sadness.

No—I think we were both overwhelmed by love.

Overwhelmed by forgiveness. Overwhelmed by the giftiness of confession that looks like indictment on the outside but is so counterintuitively filled with freedom on the inside. The patience and enormity and endlessness of it all. Why would God do it? Why would he save humanity through Jesus giving everything so that we could be set free?

He did it out of love.

For us.

Overwhelming love.

That perspective certainly frames our day a little differently. With thoughts of endless forgiveness as vast as the drops in the ocean filling our minds, we are free to consider more than ourselves or the moment before us, inviting mercy into the conversation.

ALONGSIDE

MERCY: Grace

It is the conversations that I've had with my kids that have been fruitful during the Peace Project.

I talk to my kids about grace—you know, when they have so much going on, I tell them to give themselves grace. I've never thought about grace being a part of mercy. Until now.

Which makes me think that in some ways I do have mercy—which I never thought I had. And that thought has inspired me, rather than let me shrug it off like I'm a lost cause.

—AP—

TKM How have you practiced?
What have you learned?

Forgiveness is not an occasional act, it is a constant attitude.

DR. MARTIN LUTHER KING JR.

DAY 12

Nice

> We are each made for goodness, love and compassion. Our lives are transformed as much as the world is when we live with these truths.
>
> DESMOND TUTU

Opportunities to practice thankfulness, kindness, and mercy abound. They present themselves almost anywhere, pretty much every day. I've been a bit surprised at how available they are. They can take almost any situation and make it better. The realization hit me the other day when I was going to Birdie's school for a schoolwide meeting.

Things involving the whole school make it easy to compare, to feel included or excluded, to feel underdressed or overdressed or better dressed. Aren't such comparisons the scattered thoughts that come with any large gathering? Especially ones involving our kids.

I layered on thankfulness as I was driving up. It's good to go into those things with a full heart. *I'm grateful for our faithful old car, even though the clock doesn't work and the doors need special attention in order to lock. Grateful for all the laughter that has gone on within its four doors and the great conversations and the places it has taken us.*

And then I almost instantly had the chance to practice kindness as I turned down a row in search of a parking space at about the same time someone turned in from the other end. We blinkered for the same spot. Honestly, I was happy to give the spot to them. It was a beautiful day, and even though I was late (another story of my life), I considered how I could make the most of a longer walk.

Which I did.

I lean into opportunities to practice mercy, many of which take place in my thoughts.

Lots of good occurs at schools around the world. But challenging and unavoidable hardships also lurk in the halls at every school, on every playground, and in every gymnasium. With five kids, we have seen and experienced a lot.

Opportunities to practice mercy at gatherings run plentiful, since we can show mercy toward others as well as ourselves. Though taking on schooling and parenting can feel like we're in a game against each other, we're actually all in it together. Competition's *against* may carry a megaphone. But cooperation's *alongside*, though quiet, is bigger and more powerful.

And *together* is beautiful. It shines a light on the fact that, in general, people are nice.

Maybe that's one of the sweetest aspects of practicing thankfulness, kindness, and mercy; it opens our eyes to the ever-present beauty around us. It takes something seemingly ordinary and brings it center stage to celebrate extraordinary.

After the assembly at Birdie's school, while I was slowly making my way toward a walk-up pickup line, rather than a drive-through, I capitalized on every opportunity to talk to those around me. For me, one of a schoolwide meeting's major perks is people. People and chatting. I have become my mother.

"Oh, Kay!" our ever-sweet and delightful school receptionist stopped me as I walked by her desk on my way to get Birdie.

"Hi, Cindy." I smiled back at her.

"Kay, I think this key might be yours?"

Huh? A key?

She rustled through some papers on her desk, then lifted a single car key stuck to the underside of a yellow Post-it Note bearing "KAY" in black Sharpie.

I looked at the key, realized it was my own, and wondered how in the world it had ended up at Cindy's desk. The last I knew I had put it in my pocket after locking the car. I have to manually lock it these days because of a blown fuse.

"That sure is my key," I remarked, still wondering how she had gotten it. I couldn't help but also wonder how many times Cindy has had this conversation with me.

"Someone thought you might be missing it, so they brought it to me." She laughed and shrugged. There's never a judgmental bone in her body, only kind words of encouragement. She's simply nice. "I'm just glad you've got it."

I was dumbfounded—not only about how it could have happened but also how someone could have noticed and been so incredibly nice to pick it up and get it to a safe place. Seriously—a single key. It could have been anywhere along my path. It would have taken hours for me to retrace every step I took in order to find it.

I was floored and deeply moved by the kindness of the whole thing.

Why can't kindness rule our days? Why not celebrate and sink into quiet "nice" instead of letting loud "rude" steal the show?

Like gratitude, focusing on kindness is a win-win for everyone, even bystanders. The nice person who found my key, who I'd later learn to be a parent from Birdie's class, left a buried treasure of goodness that blessed Cindy, Birdie, and me. The key-returner made quite the impact with one simple act.

Nice crosses our paths every day, but it often goes unnoticed. Though it shouldn't. Noticing and calling out nice, and being grateful for it, fuels its soul-power to change our day.

After saying goodbye to Cindy, I got Birdie and his friend who were coming over from their class, and we headed to the car. I smiled as my key slid into the ignition. We got home and, as if on cue, an opportunity to notice nice presented itself again in the most unlikely place—our mail.

While most mail consists of advertisements, fliers, more ads masquerading as magazines, political mailers, a few bills, and a lot of junk, I was surprised to see a large, white envelope hand-addressed to me in the stack. Not the fake hand-addressed that clever mass marketers use to trick us into opening an envelope. This was real.

So I opened it. And to my surprise, I pulled out a *Good Grit* magazine, autographed by the cover artist, with a thank-you note for my subscription. What?! Who does that?

Some super nice people from the South, that's who.

I had never heard of *Good Grit* until it caught my eye a few weeks before as I checked out at our grocery store and noticed my sister's dear friend Shelly on the cover. I bought it for my sister, snapped and sent a pic, then decided to read it before mailing it off to her, which I'm not sure I ever did—a nice thought stopped from action by procrastination. I really enjoyed the magazine, so I subscribed. I think what they do is cool and happy and interesting. We can all use a little of those things. I already thought they were nice people over there at *Good Grit* magazine—now I knew. They had a nice idea, acted on it, and made me feel special.

Which is what kindness does—makes people feel special. It's powerful. And I love it.

Then later that week I received another package in the mail. *What in the world?! More nice people.*

This time a shirt was inside a white hand-addressed envelope from Chatbooks, a service that compiles photos into simple books. I barely had time to hold the shirt up before one of my kids snatched it. Had I recently ordered a Chatbook? No. It was a thank-you gift and note for the ordering I'd done in the past. And let's just say I'm not a huge customer. I simply used them as an end-of-year teacher gift and a graduation party memory book for about forty seniors the year *before*. The books themselves were great. I would never have imagined to be thanked *again* months later!

Nice is everywhere.

Sometimes nice things happen on repeat, which makes them easy to overlook and treat as business as usual. But acts of kindness are not business as usual; they're special.

For several years, very nice people at Church of the Incarnation in Dallas opened their doors every week to host our neighborhood Bible study. Every week they set up a room for us with tables and chairs. They brewed fresh coffee, set out cups and ice water, and made us feel welcomed and loved. The kicker? They did it out of the kindness of their hearts, asking nothing in return, even though we weren't members of their church. They simply knew we needed a place to meet and opened their doors.

And it's not just us. They are nice, without fanfare or self-promotion, to all their neighbors, including the kids at neighboring North Dallas High School, which has one of the highest homeless student populations in North Texas. The church created an after-school drop-in center where kids are welcomed on any weekday to stop by for a meal and tutoring session in a safe place. What?! Who does that?

Nice people. People making people feel seen, cared for, and loved by simple acts of kindness. In all that seems caustic, divided, and sometimes mean, let's remember to see nice people—and, maybe more importantly, be nice people.

ALONGSIDE

PRACTICE: Experience

As you practice these things—kindness and mercy, grace and forgiveness—it goes beyond the thinking about them to experiencing them.

I never realized how often I stopped at thinking. It's the doing part that is actually changing my thinking.

SB—

TKM How have you practiced?
What have you learned?

We are each made for goodness, love and compassion. Our lives are transformed as much as the world is when we live with these truths.

DESMOND TUTU

DAY 13

The Willingness of Mercy

> That word is "willing." It's an attitude and spirit of cooperation that should permeate our conversations. It's like a palm tree by the ocean that endures the greatest winds because it knows how to gracefully bend.
>
> STEPHEN KENDRICK

We've talked about compassion and forgiveness paving mercy's road but have only touched on willingness as a key player. It's the first action in James Keenan's definition of mercy: "willingness to enter into the chaos of another."

Stepping up and out onto mercy's path can be a little unsettling as it's often hard to see beyond the first foot forward. Though mercy offers a lot of things, initial solid ground doesn't seem to be one of them. How can we get past the head and heart issues that find comfort in self-preservation and self-protection that are often at odds with mercy?

Trust.

A simple word yet a challenging prospect.

The kids and I used to have a code word for when we were teasing each other about intimidating situations: Tabasco.

Tabasco, a sweet little calico cat, used to roam around my parents' block. Their next-door neighbor fed her. And every kid on the block searched for her so they could play with her. My kids adored her. My folks? Not so much.

But despite my mother's valiant effort and the lack of a warm welcome, Tabasco spent a great amount of her day in *their* flower bed. In fact, almost every time we came to the front door, Tabasco's meows could be heard. Quick to leave her resting spot and run our direction, she would loudly announce herself all the way.

She craved attention, and the kids eagerly desired to give it to her.

But as soon as one of them would bend down to offer a gentle stroke or scratch behind her ears, Tabasco would dart away. Not far away but just out of reach. Then she would come back, again, meowing loudly as if to say, "Please don't go inside . . . just sit with me for a minute." Then she'd dart away once more to avoid a harmless outstretched hand. Then back, then away. If we would take extra time to sit for a few minutes on the porch, she would race to rub up against a back or slink into an available lap.

I found her actions so interesting. She craved connection but only on her terms. The attention and love she so longed to receive offered itself almost every time we would see her. Yet she couldn't force herself to come near unless she controlled the when and the how. She ran *from* rather than *to* the safe and gentle arms that were eager to care for her. She struggled with trust. Probably for good reason.

Some days we would take the extra time to play her game. Most days we had to move on.

"That cat sure is ridiculous," I said to Snopes as we left one day.

"Yeah," she agreed. "She so badly wants us to pet her, but she runs just far enough away to be outside of our reach."

"What a waste," chimed her brother.

But I think we're often like Tabasco, only building relationships based on our terms. We run out of reach, thinking we know best, not trusting others but resting on what we *see* rather than what we *know* to be true. When conversations, whether spoken out loud or in our heads, start to go south, it's easy to turn inward rather than be hurt. A wall goes up and we isolate ourselves. A tactic we can use even while standing next to someone.

The other day I had to call a Tabasco on myself. Walls had come up when old hurt from well-worn thought patterns revisited. Willingness to enter such territory, a place where mercy is most desperately needed, can be hard to tap. Quitting feels better. At least, momentarily.

In this particular incident, words were said at an inopportune time that knocked the breath out of me. With no time to respond, let alone process, I had to run into a meeting. The conversation, a familiar one with different verses through the years, played on in my thoughts. Even during the meeting. Making things worse, the divided thoughts held me captive from being fully present. The conversation that shut me down is an old one that leaves me sick, even though the person speaking wouldn't necessarily intend their words as mean.

It's complicated.

Since significant life challenges were already on a repeating playlist in my mind, I did momentarily check out. I built a wall that felt like protection. But I've lived long enough to know that such walls are bricked with bitterness rather than betterment. Such walls can become protective prisons that require lots of managing, which in turn tethers our thoughts to ourselves, not a great place to be.

Here's where willingness comes in.

If I can get to the whys behind both sides of the conversation—as in, why the misgivings, the uneasiness, or bad feelings and what has been going on to prompt them—I can reach for willingness to engage rather than run. The whys can help me own my part. And with my part healthily owned, I can genuinely find compassion and work toward forgiveness.

The hard part is practicing mercy without assuming victim-status or allowing someone to walk all over us. I think that's only possible when we own our identity as declared by God rather than let it be informed by what others say or do to us.

So I try.

Grabbing hold of thankfulness that stands ever ready to put our thoughts in the right place, we can try to return harsh implications and even words (coming from wounded, hurt, and afraid people) with kindness fueled by mercy. So I decided to apologize for checking out and isolating myself during the meeting. Not in the moment but after I had time to gather my bearings and point myself in a productive direction. Since trying is best done together, I ran it by Jon.

"Aren't you just inviting yourself to be hurt again?" he asked after I told him my plan.

"Maybe, but I think that owning my part and reaching for mercy will actually lead to less hurt. Maybe it'll even help me not to get hurt if, or when, it comes up again in the future." Which I'm guessing it will, since it has for so long.

"I'm not so sure," he said.

Then we talked through the whys on the other side. Hurt people hurt people. That is not an excuse, but it can help us get to compassion. We are all products of well-intentioned misinformation and painful past experiences. We can extend mercy and practice kindness with an understanding of hardship or past hurts in someone's life because we've been there too.

Getting our thoughts in the right place to be able to healthily engage with mercy can be quite a challenge. Corrie ten Boom, author and Holocaust survivor, lived this on more than one occasion. She shared her famous story of coming face-to-face with a ruthless concentration camp guard years after the war had ended. He approached her after she had spoken at an event he attended. Her blood froze as he apologized for what he had done at Ravensbrück, then asked her forgiveness. Knowing that "forgiveness is an act of the will, and the will can function regardless of the temperature of the heart," she reached for willingness and conjured up courage and acted.[1] The resulting peace overwhelmed her.

So later in life, as she faced the prospect of forgiving friends whom she loved for something they did that hurt her, she was surprised that willingness darted out of reach.

> You would have thought that, having forgiven the Nazi guard, this would have been child's play. It wasn't. For weeks I seethed inside. But at last I asked God again to work His miracle in me. And again it happened: first the cold-blooded decision, then the flood of joy and peace.
>
> . . . Then, why was I suddenly awake in the middle of the night, hashing over the whole affair again? My *friends*! I thought. *People I loved!* If it had been strangers, I wouldn't have minded so.[2]

She prayed again for willingness to forgive, then confessed her struggle to a Lutheran pastor friend. He gave her a gentle response that was filled with compassion and hope. He compared forgiveness to bells in a church tower rung by the pulling of a rope. When the bell ringer stops pulling, the bells still ring as they swing, then slow to a stop.

> "I believe the same thing is true of forgiveness. When we forgive someone, we take our hand off the rope. But if we've been tugging at our grievances for a long time, we mustn't be surprised if the old angry thoughts keep coming for a while. They're just the ding-dongs of the old bell slowing down."
>
> And so it proved to be. There were a few more midnight reverberations, a couple of dings when the subject came up in my conversation. But the force—which was my willingness in the matter—had gone out of them. They came less and less often and at last stopped altogether.[3]

Willingness can be used to hang on to grudges, to be resentful, to give in to bitterness. Or willingness can be accessed to forgive, to meet someone where they are, to find compassion by recognizing that their chaos isn't unique to them. I have chaos too. I may need to go a step further to remember that the bells from my own issues may still be reverberating for someone I harmed.

And maybe I, too, can learn, as Corrie did, a secret of forgiveness: "that we can trust God not only above our emotions, but also above our thoughts."[4]

Willingness is a key player in our practice of mercy.

It hinges on trust. Even, maybe especially, when we can't see everything that might authenticate and warrant trust. This circles back to where we are placing our faith. What is the object of trust? Will it be our fear, anxieties, or worries? Or will it be God?

I think about Tabasco and her trust issues as compared with my trust issues. The greatest difference is their source. Tabasco's source is fickle people. My source is love that is absolute and supreme, completely trustworthy—*ultimate* love, acceptance, and protection. In seeking, considering, and choosing to sink into that truth, we can lead with the fact that we have been made right (made righteous) and have nothing to prove.

Then, anchored in and bolstered by the certainty of our okayness, we can willingly trust the solid ground on which we stand. Fully aware that someone else's chaos (agenda, insecurities, stress, pressures, fears, or history) has little bearing upon us, we can practice mercy rather than pull back and race for the security of the front bushes.

The willingness part of mercy comes into play when we step out in trust. And comparison quits when we realize that everyone has chaos—that all of us have been hurt or have hurt others.

In Brian Stevenson's book *Just Mercy*, he does such an outstanding job outlining one of the most compelling reasons for willingness—the fact that we are all in this together. Everyone is broken.

He shares wisdom from monk, theologian, and author Thomas Merton:

> The writer Thomas Merton said: "We are bodies of broken bones." I guess I'd always known but never fully considered that being broken is what makes us human. We all have our reasons. Sometimes we're fractured by the choices we make; sometimes we're shattered by things we would never have chosen. But our brokenness is also the source of our common humanity, the basis for our shared search for comfort, meaning, and healing. Our shared vulnerability and imperfection nurtures and sustains our capacity for compassion.
>
> We have a choice. We can embrace our humanness, which means embracing our broken natures and the compassion that remains our best hope for healing. Or we can deny our brokenness, forswear compassion, and, as a result, deny our own humanity.[5]

"Being broken is what makes us human." Yes. And we have a choice.

Could it be that in seeing the brokenness around us we can deal with the brokenness within us? In the willingness part of mercy, maybe we can find our belovedness, a hard thing to believe about ourselves. Theologian Henri Nouwen honestly addressed it well:

> I kept running around it in large or small circles, always looking for someone or something able to convince me of my Belovedness. Self-rejection is the greatest enemy of the spiritual life because it contradicts the sacred voice that calls us the "Beloved." Being the Beloved expresses the core truth of our existence.[6]

Recognizing that "core truth of our existence"—the worthiness that far exceeds any thoughts we could think about ourselves—invites compassion into the process and provides the spark we need in order to be willing. We can walk toward someone in confidence, independent of their reaction, in the safety from which we operate as Beloved. Trusting the one who declares us to be beloved.

It is in acting upon such trust that core truths become real and take on life, especially things of the heart and of the soul. Maybe as we acknowledge belovedness in others through the genuine practice of mercy, the seeds will be fertilized within our own soul.

TKM How have you practiced?
What have you learned?

That word is "willing." It's an attitude and spirit of cooperation that should permeate our conversations. It's like a palm tree by the ocean that endures the greatest winds because it knows how to gracefully bend.

STEPHEN KENDRICK

DAY 14

Lightness of Being

> Sweet mercy is nobility's true badge.
>
> WILLIAM SHAKESPEARE

This Peace Project was a feast, but it might end up being more of a cleanse, as in a soul-cleanse, because that's what seems to be going on. Something deep at a soul-level is happening.

A levity has entered our sphere.

"Have you been doing our little Soul30 thing?" I asked Snopes when we were almost at the halfway point of our experiment.

"Yes," she said. "Sometimes in my head instead of always writing it down."

Just that she's thinking about it is wonderful. And I love that she feels the freedom to write or not write her experience down. Getting caught up in checking some box or getting it done just to do it sort of misses the point. I'm not a fan of the performance gospel that says you have to do in order to be okay.

A friend told me, "This is not a to-do thing but more of a God-doing-through-me thing." Which is a nice way to think about it because that just might be the source of levity: experiencing the mystery of God working through us.

"Have you noticed a levity?" I asked the friend. "I mean, it seems like, with the boys, with all of us, a lightness is there."

"I know," she said—almost wide-eyed. "Absolutely."

"We're not making this up?"

"No." She seemed as moved by it as me. "It's really there." Then she added, "I find myself thinking about it all the time. Honestly—it's mercy that has really impacted my thoughts."

Me too. Even when I need help seeing it. The night before the conversation with my friend, the kids had stopped me in my tracks, floating the *mercy* word my way (again) when I was frustrated about an inconvenience. It was silly and involved someone we love.

"I'm grateful you guys pointed out the opportunities to have mercy," I told them the following morning. "You were right last night. As soon as I grabbed it, I think we all felt peace enter the picture."

When someone is frustrated, everyone feels it in the same way that everyone feels peace when it arrives on the scene. Since we've been purposefully seeking opportunities to practice mercy, it is now much easier to see and to do—genuinely. That night it touched each person in the car, especially the one who had unwittingly caused the frustration.

Mercy invited dignity to all of us by inviting respect and worth rather than giving in to temptations to treat someone like an object. And how fascinating to see the undeniable power of mercy almost the instant it was tapped.

I think it goes back to Dr. Evans' illustration of a chain with things like anger, frustration, resentment, and bitterness as the links. Well, those and their friends fear, anxiety, and worry. Those feelings had me tied up when the kids prompted me toward mercy.

It was a typical night at the end of a regular day, the kind where curveballs out of nowhere peppered the path, where emails were received regarding issues that needed immediate attention, where the fun part of procrastination was replaced by the stress of all that still needed to be done but hadn't been. Not all our regular days look like that since we're blank-space people—we like blank calendars, not busy ones—but busy days are normal days because stuff happens.

So dinner needed to be grabbed rather than cooked. And that's where the engine on internal misgivings started. On the way to get hamburgers for a couple, chicken nuggets for one, and tacos for another—yes, I'm a short-order drive-through cook (your mercy for today can be not judging me)—we realized that a cousin without a car was in town and staying at my folks' place. So I called to see if we could pick him up a hamburger.

"That would be great!" he told us. "A double cheeseburger, some fries, and a Coke would be awesome."

Done. Good feelings from kindness poured in.

"We're on our way, so we'll drop it off in about fifteen minutes."

"I'll come out and grab it," he said. Then added, "In fact, I'll come over and eat with y'all, if that's okay."

"Perfect." Even better.

In the background of my thoughts, having nothing to do with him, was a tiny bit of unspoken pressure to make this a quick run. It was really pressure I had put on myself to have a fresh hamburger and fries back to our house for Jon since he likes his food hot. I knew he wouldn't say a word about it and would be happy to use the microwave, but I also knew it had been a long workday for him too. And I felt some unspoken burden to walk in with a hot rather than cold burger.

With that weighing on my mind, we made our rounds. Chicken nuggets first, tacos second, burgers last. There weren't even lines. All was fine in the world until we swung by to pick up the recipient of a meal that had made us all happy.

I texted him as we pulled into the back drive. "We're here."

Then we waited.

One of the kids texted. "Hey—we've got your dinner."

Silence.

"Someone call," I said. I was starting to get nervous about the hamburgers getting cold and worried about the frustration Jon might feel at home. That may sound ridiculous, but I was feeling it. I guess I had already had a few bouts with expectation-stress in other areas during my day.

Still silence. No answer or return text. So I got out of the car—a little huffy—muttering on about all the ick that would meet us on the other side of a cold burger. I even added a few dramatic exaggerations involving words like *always* and *never*—and ran into the house. "WE'RE HERE!"

Which is when I heard the shower and realized it might be a few minutes. As I got back in the car a little frustrated, the kids hit me with "Mercy, Mom."

"It's a hamburger." My shotgun rider gently offered some perspective.

And he was right. Our dinner guest had no idea we were trying to race home. Why would he? We are consistently laid-back. We would soon find out he just wanted to take a quick shower after exercising. And he was quick.

So, as mercy did what it always does—dialed down intensity and invited peace—those chains were broken. The links lost their power. A sense of levity and dignity for everyone involved appeared. Just as folks walking alongside a frustrated person can't help but field the emotional shrapnel and feel the heaviness, everyone gets to experience the gentle waves of peace in the midst of mercy.

Maybe it's because, in the depth of our being, we crave grace. And when we're in its presence, it's like a sweet reminder of what we've been made for. Grace given and grace received acts like a blast of pure oxygen from above, invigorating the air we breathe with life reminders.

In that moment, grace invited worthiness to the human beings around me. One had no idea we might be in a hurry and innocently grabbed a quick shower. One held hostage by a ticking clock was set free when she realized that a lukewarm hamburger is not that big of a deal. We all know what long days can do to a person. And a few of my innocent bystanders, whose joy in a simple act of kindness was stripped when I let stress steal the show, invited it back by very kindly offering perspective and walking the road alongside me. They gently reminded me that a lifeline to extend mercy sits ever-present in all moments.

Rather than links of resentment, frustration, or bitterness, mercy's chain is comprised exclusively of compassion and grace—links that are strong and never break, and when used, gain strength and remind us of their source: eternal compassion and grace that stand ready to claim victory in any moment.

TKM How have you practiced? What have you learned?

Sweet mercy is nobility's true badge.

WILLIAM SHAKESPEARE

DAY 15

A Person's Chaos

> Amnesty is as good for those who give it as for those who receive it. It has the admirable quality of bestowing mercy on both sides.
>
> VICTOR HUGO

"I do but don't want to practice kindness."

"Same." Snopes sighed.

I think we were tired.

Snopes and I had just dropped off Birdie when I got a text from someone who needed a ride. We had offered help to a friend who was in town for a few months anytime she needed it. But when the call for help came, it hit both of us the wrong way. We were in the middle of last-minute runs before dinner.

Hey—can y'all come get me? I need to go back to school to grab something.

Sure, but we have to run a couple of places before we can get there. Where are you now?

OMW home with a friend.

Can they drop you back at school?

No.

Pause.

I guess I'll just find another ride. The school closes at 5:30—so never mind.

The text had a slight tone, but we certainly could have been reading into it. Honestly, reading my response back now—I'm sure I came across a little passive-aggressive.

Ok—well, we will just come now.

Ah . . . text talk. Such a fun endeavor. Especially at the end of a long day.

There were issues (chaos), as there always are, that neither of us knew about the other. For our friend, the week had been rocky. She had forgotten something she needed and thought that the forgotten item would cause a lot of unnecessary anguish the next day. For us, we had to pick up a car from the shop before it closed, grab dinner on the other side of town, and get back in time to be descended upon by an energized group of seventh graders for their small group meeting as it was our month to host.

Welcome to chaos.

According to Michael Formica with *Psychology Today*, there are basically two types of human chaos: internal and external.

> Internal chaos runs the gamut from personal idiosyncrasy, to the voices in our head, to our ambient anxiety, to the various versions of dysfunction or disorder that we drag around with us from day to day. These things are part of the fabric of our personality. . . .
>
> External chaos comes from the outside . . . [like] the driver who makes a right hand turn from the left hand lane. . . . Things

> like this are pretty much out of our control and are, more than anything else, simply visited upon us.[1]

A mix of internal and external chaos had hit us all that day, and some of it was intersecting with the others.

Our chaos, in the form of destinations across town from each other coupled with internal anxiety and angst over another person's perceived reaction, likely had us all on edge. On another day my response would have been lathered in *whatever-works-best-for-you*—genuinely.

Some internal chaos is long-lived and deeply rooted. Sometimes we are unaware of the chaos simply because those roots are comfortable and seem reasonable as we have lost sight of what life was like without the added weight. Some chaos comes with age. Old can equal cranky or flaky (no comment from the kid gallery) in the same way toddlers "need a nap." Other chaos comes with physiological stages, stresses of a day, past baggage, pressures we put on ourselves or feel from others—the list goes on. And honestly, rarely do we see the chaos for what it really is. No one wears a sign announcing it. We get so comfortable in it, we don't recognize it as chaos.

Like so much else in life, it gets even more complicated, possibly exponentially more complicated, as lives intersect. But as Mr. Formica points out,

> The truth is, we are surrounded by mirrors, and, if we can see what's going on in someone else's life, we should—with a little effort and a little humility—be able to recognize it in ourselves.[2]

And in recognizing chaos in ourselves as well as others, we can gain freedom through the powerful acts of compassion and grace that form mercy. Which is where Snopes and I sat, face-to-face with the day's chaos and our own willingness (or lack thereof) to enter into it.

We had offered to help anytime, and we genuinely wanted to. So we not only determined to have happy hearts in an effort toward kindness but also to practice mercy and understanding. We chose to receive that text, which may have indeed had a layer of tone, with understanding.

Lately I've been contemplating the willingness part of mercy, trying to understand how to practice it without posturing as a victim or feeling used or holding a grudge. I was glad for the opportunity to try.

"I'm in for helping," I told Snopes. "But I'm also going to bring up the stuff we needed to get done." I really wanted to learn how to practice mercy without putting myself in a place where I felt like I was being walked on. I added, "I genuinely want to help, but in a way where we respect our day too."

"Please don't," she begged me.

"Oh, I will."

"No, please. That is not going to go well."

"I'm doing it." I looked over at her with a hold-on-to-your-hat expression on my face, as these were uncharted waters.

Normally we stuff down hurt feelings and keep going, figuring it's not a big deal. But we can address any issues in the name of mercy and allow it to work the wonders that it had been working during our experiment. I wanted to grab roots before they went bitter, even if only a tiny bit bitter.

Snopes cringed. We pulled up as our friend came out, looking a bit frazzled.

"Hey," Snopes and I nervously said at the same time.

"Hi," she replied, distracted. "Thanks for coming."

Something was up.

"You okay?" I asked. "Is everything all right? We had to drop a few things to run over, but you're important to us and it doesn't look like everything is okay." I attempted to out our changed plans while hitting home why we wanted to change them. Mainly that she means more to us than changed plans.

"It's not," she replied.

"Can you tell us? Really—we rearranged things because you're worth it. Maybe we can help."

She sighed. "I'm sorry." And then the tears came.

The stress of her situation was heavy on her heart. The last thing she ever wanted was to be a burden, so asking us to help was a big deal. The only way for her to handle the situation was going back to school, and she knew the doors would be locked by 5:30 p.m. She didn't want to chance Uber, but she felt silly for being upset and really didn't want to put anyone out as the issue was her fault—at least in her mind. Cue the brutal mindsight that truly was anything but 20/20 in this situation.

And in the craziest way, because we had lightly come clean about our own issues, she had a green light to share hers and invite us in. We quickly reframed the things she felt were happening, showering her with truth.

"They love you at that school. Oh my goodness—you couldn't do anything to disappoint them." This friend is seriously lovable.

She had forgotten to take home movie passes that a teacher couldn't use. He had made such a production of leaving them taped on his door for her, the thought of him returning to find them still there was too much. His certain frustration at her for presumed ungratefulness kept playing over in her mind, working her up into panic mode. And thus prompting her to text us.

"Honestly, if he saw the tickets, he wouldn't care," I said to her. "He wouldn't have given them to you if he had wanted them. And he knows you can use them anytime. He gave them to you because he likes you, not to get mad at you."

With those truthful words, the entire scenario changed.

Even though we started out simply going through the motions since our hearts were only half there, mercy still barreled in like a hero on a white horse, saving both of us from our misperceptions and restoring places we didn't realize needed restoring. With compassion leading the way, any resentments, misgivings, or frustrations instantly receded for each of us. Disappeared, in fact. And we could happily head over to the school. Even our being late getting home was nothing.

And truth be told, any hurt feelings and misgivings have yet to find their way back into our relationship (or our texts).

Mercy continues to surprise us.

ALONGSIDE

PURE KINDNESS: Freedom

I'm not sure I've ever thought about the complicated aspect of kindness and of people.

The Peace Project has been showing me things about myself that I didn't know. And it has brought freedom along with it. Like what comes with pure kindness, not even messed up by me.

I've discovered that I even can mess with kindness, making it more about myself than being nice. I've realized that sometimes I'm being kind in order to look good or get something for me. What?!

We people are complicated. Probably 99.9999 percent of the complication is our obsession with ourselves and control.

—TJ—

TKM How have you practiced?
What have you learned?

Amnesty is as good for those who give it as for those who receive it.
It has the admirable quality of bestowing mercy on both sides.

VICTOR HUGO

DAY 16

Kindness without Consequence

> Three things in human life are important: the first is to be kind; the second is to be kind; and the third is to be kind.
>
> HENRY JAMES

"Do you mind if I ask you a question?" Eleanor, a nice cashier, asked Snopes and me.

"Sure," I responded.

"Great. Okay." She checked to see if anyone was in line, then fired her question. "So if you could have any superpower—any—what would you pick and how would you use it?"

I think Snopes and I were a little taken aback, though not too much since we absolutely love any chance to talk to someone. Or at least I do. (I have a talking disorder, as in overtalking.) The thing about Eleanor's question that surprised me was where we were when she asked—at the drive-through window at Starbucks.

It was toward the end of a rainy day, so maybe the lines had been light. Eleanor, whom we had seen a few times as we've driven through, was making the most of her opportunity for extended time with customers. What an unexpected and fun question. Especially the second part.

"Hmm . . ." We both paused. "Superpower," I repeated, trying to land on just the right one. Because you only get one.

Eleanor leaned out the window again. "Looks like y'all have thought about this before," she commented.

"Yes," I said, "but your 'what would you do with it?' takes it a bit deeper."

"Right?" she replied.

"Okay." I took a deep breath. I had kindness and the power that we've all seen in its wake on my brain, especially the way it makes everyone in the equation feel so great. "So, not to sound cheesy, but I think I would like some sort of power to be able to know what's going on in someone's life to best be able to show them kindness. I mean, being kind makes everyone feel good. It would be fun to be able to do that all the time. Being able to meet a specific need but without knowing *everything* in someone's life, you know? Something like that."

"Yeah," Eleanor replied, nodding. "I'm going to riff on yours a little. What if you could have kindness with no consequences?"

"Yesss!" Snopes chimed in.

"Wait, say that again." I was slow on the uptake.

"Kindness without consequences," Eleanor repeated. "So that kindness overflows without a depletion of resources for the giver and no taking it a wrong way or anything else for the receiver. So there never has to be an end to the goodness. And that it's covered in safe boundaries."

"Oh yes," Snopes agreed. "I've thought about that before. You can help anytime without worries."

"Wow, I love that," I agreed, still letting it sink in. What a great idea. My mind raced with the possibilities of this "superpower." Endless resources to offer kindness from a bottomless well, even within our soul. Kindness with every aspect covered—finances, time, physical and emotional safety—so we never feel taken advantage of. Where kindness is received and given in absolute freedom. With no agendas, just simple care and love on both sides.

I liked this game.

"Can we ask you back?" Snopes inquired.

"Oh—like what my superpower would be?" Eleanor peeked to the line behind us again. We had time to continue.

"Yes, what would you choose?" I asked.

"I would have universal multilingualism. The ability to know all languages, every species, plants and animals, everything. I would love to be able to understand, communicate, and translate without boundaries."

Of course she would. What a caring and kind superpower.

The question about a superpower isn't new. My kids play it often with their friends and cousins. Eleanor took it a significant step further. Adding the altruistic element to something that could easily be self-serving reminds me that it's the "how it could be used" that connects us to humanity.

She handed us our order and encouraged us to ask people her question if we had the opportunity.

"If you ask a lot of people that question," she told us, "you can get some insight on people's dreams and hopes and fears."

We wished each other a nice afternoon and went on about our day.

"I loved all of that," Snopes said dreamily as we drove away. "Her superpower. The kindness with no consequences. All of it."

"Me too," I replied, still lingering in all the possibilities. "People are amazing."

The idea of kindness without consequences is a reminder that even acts of kindness can prove complicated.

I love the poem titled "Anyway" by Kent Keith. Because it was one of Mother Teresa's favorites, she had it written on the wall of her home for children in Calcutta. It points to several positive practices, including forgiving people no matter where they're coming from, doing good whether or not people notice or remember.

And it goes on to encourage brave, noble efforts regardless of the response. "If you are kind, people may accuse you of selfishness, ulterior motives. Do good anyway."[1]

Such strange consequences for the other side of kind. And how unusual for Mother Teresa to speak of them. I wonder if people accused her of selfish, ulterior motives.

Maybe that's where mercy comes into play. Looking for and landing on compassion for people who would not only think that way, but quite possibly practice kindness for their personal gain, basically ruining the altruistic rush that kindness consistently washes over the giver.

Kindness does not mean being a doormat, the same way mercy does not mean being a victim. Maybe kindness and mercy both come with the need to recognize people may use them to their advantage. But with our worth firmly anchored in God's declaration, we can stand solid.

According to author Tony Fahkry, "You should in no way undermine your self-worth at the expense of others, but simply practice kindness while upholding your integrity." He then added a quote from author Matt Kahn, who states:

> When human interactions become a way of practicing self-acceptance by treating others with more patience, kindness, and respect, a constant need to be heard shifts into listening as an act of love.[2]

Kindness without consequence. Listening as an act of love. A few things worth thinking about and acting upon. All with heightened awareness of what we can learn about ourselves and others.

How fun that we got to think about such a deep subject at a Starbucks drive-through.

Kindness opens the door to knowing someone, and it leads to someone possibly feeling known. Maybe that's when its benefits come and put consequence on the back burner.

ALONGSIDE

SUPERPOWER: No Fear

Maybe the superpower I would want is no fear from things that I really shouldn't fear. Cool to think about what my life would look like if I didn't have a fear of fellow humans. There are healthy fears. But I would choose to have no *unhealthy* fears.

Then I thought about what I would do with it. And I would be bolder. Well, truth be told, I already have that superpower in me.

—CT—

TKM How have you practiced?
What have you learned?

Three things in human life are important: the first is to be kind; the second is to be kind; and the third is to be kind.

HENRY JAMES

DAY 17

Surprised by Gratitude

> To be grateful is to recognize the Love of God in everything He has given us—and He has given us everything. Every breath we draw is a gift of His love, every moment of existence is a grace, for it brings with it immense graces from Him.
>
> Gratitude therefore takes nothing for granted, is never unresponsive, is constantly awakening to new wonder and to praise of the goodness of God. For the grateful person knows that God is good, not by hearsay but by experience.
>
> And that is what makes all the difference.
>
> THOMAS MERTON

Sometimes a heightened awareness of steadfast truth and love can come on like a surprise party when least expected. The door opens and out pours a flood of realization and humble gratitude—overwhelmed by thankfulness.

I had it in spades this weekend. I barely knew what hit me. But I'm so glad it did.

Pulling up the address for Fury's district swim meet prompted memories. Seeing the Don Rodenbaugh Natatorium in Allen, Texas, come up on my phone's map as the location connected with the address made me chuckle.

Apparently, life actually does come full circle.

When the kids were little, I kept my eyes peeled and ears tuned in for fun things, preferably indoors, to do in the summer. The dollar movies, a cool archery range close to our house, the practice putting green at Dick's Sporting Goods (it was free, and they were nice to let us use it).

We would use any excuse to ride the DART train. We especially loved riding downtown to the Plaza of the Americas station to grab a bite of lunch at the food court with Jon and enjoy watching the people ice-skating on their indoor rink. Every so often the kids would rent skates and join in the fun.

But the Don Rodenbaugh Natatorium in Allen was one of our favorite places. It's a bit of a drive but worth the splurge. The lazy river and waterslides provided hours of entertainment. I used to sit and watch as the kids splashed around. And I'd sometimes look over to catch local swim teams practicing and wonder if any of my kids would join the swim team when they were old enough. My dad encouraged—otherwise known as *made*—my siblings and me to competitively swim for at least three years each. Since he learned to swim as an adult, it was important to him that we each knew how to swim well at a young age. We might have complained, but it was actually a gift. My older brother was a ranked swimmer, so we frequented swim meets. It's such a beautiful sport. I nostalgically hoped one of mine would come to love it too.

Fury is that kid.

So there I sat, scrunched next to other parents on wet bleachers, reminiscing about those little-kid days where I'd peek over at the lane-swimmers while my little ones enjoyed freely splashing about on the other side of the natatorium.

I also caught myself remembering back to this time a year ago. Things were a bit different. Fury's story had taken quite an unexpected detour. It began with one of those phone calls you never want to receive.

I had just returned to Dallas after spending some time in Arizona with my girls and my folks. The girls and I had driven a car out to them and stayed for a few days. It was great, but I was glad to be home with our boys. All except for Fury, who had gone skiing with Young Life.

My boy who usually shies away from group things was one of the first to sign up for the ski trip. With so many in our family, mountain getaways usually don't land on the front burner since they can be a bit pricey.

But Fury has always loved a good adventure. He's the kid who you might find outside, jumping off the roof onto the trampoline, barefoot in shorts while it's snowing.

He's tough and rarely complains. For example, when he was in third grade, an accident on the playground equipment landed him in the ER, blood-soaked and with a cracked head. I watched as my gritty kid sat still while having his head stapled with botched pain medicine. He would hold up his hand after the click of the stapler met his scalp, inhale and exhale deeply, then say, "Okay, do the next one," rather than wait for the doctor to come fix the numbing issue. "I can do this," he had confidently told me.

That's kind of his mantra. I always wonder what the good Lord has planned for him.

With Fury out of town on his ski-trip adventure, I was spending some quality time with Birdie, who was working on his latest artsy creation. Then the phone rang.

Our Young Life area director's number popped up. Initial thoughts raced to a form I must have forgotten (usually the case), but at the same time, I felt a tiny sense of dread and braced myself like I do with those calls from school.

"Kay?" Robert said, then dove right in. "I just wanted to let you know that Fury had an accident. He's doing better. Can I put the medic on the phone?"

"Of course," I replied, not sure, but trusting.

He handed the phone over.

"Hello? Hi, this is ski patrol. We've managed to calm your son. He's breathing now. And we need your permission to work on him. Do we have your permission?"

"Of course. Yes," I replied, though I wasn't sure what they were talking about. "Calmed? Breathing now? Is he okay? What happened?" Now my heart was pumping. This wasn't a good phone call. It was one of the ones you hate. The kind where you take a deep breath, try to slow your pulse, and fight to rise to the occasion because you must.

The ski patrol medic answered my questions with facts. *He couldn't breathe. He's breathing now. He's been in a serious accident. With your permission to work on him, we can know more.*

"Okay." Then I asked to talk to Fury, so they handed the phone to him. The second they did, I regretted that I asked.

"Mom." He was gasping. He could barely talk. "It hurts," he whimpered while trying to breathe.

The gritty kid who barely blinked when he cracked his head open at nine could barely get the words out at sixteen. I heard the fear and pain in his voice and wished I hadn't asked to talk to him. As reality rushed in, I struggled to find my footing.

"Sweetheart, it's going to be okay," I assured him. Shaking, I didn't know what to say. "Honey, can you hand the phone back to Robert?"

"Hi," Robert began.

"He needs something for the pain," I urged. "*Please* get him something for the pain *now*." I took a deep breath. "What happened?"

"He had a pretty bad fall. His snowboard. The tip got caught. He face-planted and his legs propelled all the way over his head.

Russell, his leader, was with him and is here right now. Let me let you talk to the doc."

"Mrs. Wyma," the doc started, "your son has a contusion on his frontal lobe, as well as compression and burst fractures in vertebrae. His spinal cord appears unaffected, but we would like to send him by ambulance to Denver Health, a Trauma One facility that is fully equipped to handle this. Are you okay with us sending him to Denver?"

"Yes, of course."

"Good," the nice doc replied then handed the phone back to Robert as the wheels were set in motion.

After hanging up on the unexpected phone call, my family and I quickly started taking next steps. The first few being travel arrangements to meet Fury in Denver. A Southwest Airlines flight was set to depart in an hour. I nabbed a seat on the plane and headed to Love Field Airport. As I pulled into a parking place, grabbed my hastily packed bag, and raced for my plane, any interrupted plans seemed trivial in the moment.

An unexpected phone call replaced certainties with open-ended unknowns. But truth be told, calm surrounded the situation. A steadfast peace was dampened by a few sad tears, and whispered *I don't knows* were bathed in repeated *thank-yous* and restful *I trust you, Lords*.

I arrived at the hospital a little over an hour after Fury's ambulance did. And the amazing ER doc, Christian, walked into his room not ten minutes after I got there. He filled me in. Fury had T4–T6 compression and burst fractures and a frontal lobe contusion that had all but healed itself by the time they arrived. His spinal cord appeared untouched. They moved him to pediatric ICU for pain management and neuro checks.

Like clockwork, every single detail fell into place as medical and ministry personnel moved in and out of the picture like a beautiful symphony.

Our night, filled with scans and questions and pain meds, was sprinkled with multitudes of thankful utterances. *Thank you. Thank you. Thank you, Lord,* I repeated while watching Fury sleep. As I mentally replayed the day's happenings, I couldn't help but catch glimpses of what I know to be true in every situation (happy or sad): God goes before, behind, and beside us all day, every day. And he is good.

In this rare instance, we got a peek behind the veil. Here are just a few examples of the ways God went before.

- Three hours before the accident, we had made a reservation for Fury to come home early so he could be in Dallas for his cousin's wedding. It's a long story—but suffice it to say, Fury already had his flight home scheduled BEFORE anyone knew he needed it.
- Fury had chosen to pull off from his friends for a run on some less-steep slopes. Russell, his small group leader, went with him so he wouldn't be alone. Fury still doesn't remember anything about the accident since it knocked him unconscious, but he does remember Russell helping him when he came to. "What would have happened without Russell?" he contemplated in the hospital. "I'm so glad he was there."
- Like magic every detail was handled. The flights, the docs, the scans, the nurses—everything and everyone was amazing and seamless. Every hurdle that had to be cleared and test that had to be passed was, as if on some predetermined cue.
- And the cherry on top: We made it home for the wedding. Of course it would have been fine, more than fine, if we hadn't. No one, us especially, expected to be home. But like a sweet gift, we were. Fury actually attended the wedding. He was even in our family photo that my mom had used

for her annual Valentine card. Again, not a big deal, just sweet.

Every detail was perfect, including Fury's amazing nurse, Kelly, who went out searching to find a pair of shoes for him to wear home since his were left on the mountain. He wore those shoes every day for months, despite their geriatric stylings.

All the details fell into place. The custom back brace that should have taken days to get (the accident was on a Thursday afternoon) took only hours. His sitting upright and taking steps that should have been excruciating and slow-coming happened within twenty-four hours after the fall. Every neurological test was passed without a hitch.

So as I sat on the bleachers at the natatorium during Fury's meet and looked over at the waterslides and lazy river, this time from the lane side, I was a bit overcome and overwhelmed by gratitude as I watched the racers make their way to the starting blocks. Loud and proud, the announcer excitedly ticked through the athletes and their lane numbers over the PA. Whether or not Fury would be walking today could never change God's intimate care, even in those moments on the mountain when he was unconscious and barely breathing. Yet, there I sat, at Don Rodenbaugh Natatorium in Allen, watching him compete in the district meet.

I was literally moved to tears with gratitude. Last year we were overwhelmed by the fluke snowboard accident that led to a broken back, lots of prayers, and eventually the feeling of being SO thankful he could walk. I'm grateful for this sport that the doctors all but exclusively credited as the reason he is walking, and swimming, today. I'm not sure I really had a good cry last year over the detour from the sport we both love.

So I cried that day in the parking lot as I left the meet. Sobbing tears of gratitude—for so much.

They were a reminder to linger and to ruminate with gratitude every day because life goes so fast. A reminder to rest each day in the complete protection and provision of God, whether seen or unseen, remaining steadfast and certain in him who is good. And a reminder to be sweetly surprised by the powerful undergirding of gratitude, even through thankful tears.

TKM How have you practiced?
What have you learned?

To be grateful is to recognize the Love of God in everything
He has given us—and He has given us everything.

THOMAS MERTON

DAY 18

Keeping It Simple

> The best portion of a good man's life is his little, nameless, unremembered acts of kindness and of love.
>
> WILLIAM WORDSWORTH

As the sun rose, Mitty and I turned toward home from our walk and spied the sweetest act of kindness: a neighbor helping other neighbors by saving them a few steps and putting their papers on their porches.

It was still dark, so I could spy on her from our driveway as she made her way from one house to another and then across our street. She gathered papers from two doors down, then looked at my direct neighbor's paper. She paused for a minute because their sprinklers were going full force.

But that didn't stop her. Determined in her kindness, she reached through a sprinkler's jet of water to get and set their paper on their porch. She wasn't doing it for something in return nor to be acknowledged for a good deed. She was doing it simply to be nice. I'm afraid I interrupted the magic of her service. Not only did I see her but I spoke as well.

"That's so sweet," I said to her.

She looked up a little surprised to see someone. Then she smiled. "It's the simple things," she replied.

Yes.

The simple things.

May we never lose sight of or discount the power of something simple. The fact that kindness can be simple is all the more reason to engage in and practice it. If there's a nudge, act. Someone's life may depend on it.

Even though people might be more "connected" than ever via social media and the internet, loneliness has hit epidemic levels. Cigna recently conducted a study producing numbers to prove it true. They found that "46 percent of U.S. adults report sometimes or always feeling lonely and 47 percent report feeling left out."[1] These statistics touch on a few of our core human needs: to be known, to belong, to be accepted.

These numbers are connected to even worse stats associated with people who have thought the world would be a better place without them. Suicide is rising to all-time high levels. The loneliness trend feels overwhelming and takes us into territory we never want to travel.

What if we have within our grasp simple opportunities not to solve the issues but to make a dent in them? According to Dr. Jerry Motto at the University of California, San Francisco, simple acts of kindness can do just that.

Dr. Motto served in World War II, and the impact of writing and receiving letters while he was overseas stayed with him. They made him feel more connected to home, and that gave him a simple idea, especially after his wife, Pat Conway, said, "If you know that you are going to make a connection, and that you can communicate that you care, that's all that's important."

So Dr. Motto and some colleagues set out to see if writing letters and sending encouraging notes with the simple message that someone cares could impact people with suicidal thoughts. To their surprise, what they found was nothing short of remarkable.

In the first two years after leaving the hospital, the suicide rate of those who received Dr. Motto's caring letters was about half the rate of those who did not.[2] So can reaching out to someone—through a letter, a text, or simply touching base by using their name to acknowledge their existence and importance—make a big difference or impact the loneliness trend? Apparently it can.

Kevin Hines, a man who survived jumping from the Golden Gate Bridge, can attest to the power of caring. For Hines, the feeling of loneliness was unbearable. "All I wanted was for one person to see my pain and say something kind," he said. "I could not reach out. I needed someone to reach in."

Someone did, via a letter. And it mattered. A lot.

"Showing you care about someone—not saying it, *showing* it—is tangible. When it's tangible, it means more," he said, referring to the letters from Dr. Motto.[3]

I thought about this as I watched my neighbor quietly make her way down our street. A small act with a powerful punch. Each paper delivery sent a warm message to people she may or may not know well. It told each one that they matter. When they opened their door, they would know that someone not only thought about them but went so far as to save them a few steps in their day.

Inspired by her simple act, I texted someone who had been on my mind that I am thankful to know them, and I shared a specific way my life is better for having them in it. I couldn't have known a simple text would matter, but it did. My friend's reply: "Wow, Kay!! Thank you so, so much. I treasure these words and will read them many more times."

And I was also inspired by Queen Elizabeth's 2019 Christmas address. Coming off a year of discord in her own country and around the world, she was inspired by countries coming together to celebrate the seventy-fifth anniversary of D-Day.

> As Christmas dawned, church congregations around the world joined in singing "It Came Upon the Midnight Clear." Like many

> timeless carols, it speaks not just of the coming of Jesus Christ into a divided world many years ago but also of the relevance, even today, of the angels' message of peace and goodwill.
>
> It's a timely reminder of what positive things can be achieved when people set aside past differences and come together in the spirit of friendship and reconciliation. And, as we all look forward to the start of a new decade, it's worth remembering that it is often the small steps, not the giant leaps, that bring about the most lasting change.[4]

Yes. Simple steps.

Practicing kindness doesn't have to be big or fancy. Size and style have nothing to do with its effectiveness.

Take this morning. On our car ride to school, I had a tired chap riding shotgun. "It's going to be a terrible day," he moaned as we turned onto the street of his school.

"No." I tried to prop him up since he was too tired to fight those thoughts himself. Sometimes when we can't say no ourselves, a little help goes a long way.

Staring down what feels overwhelming can be hard to face alone. But we've learned (and lived) that choosing truth trumps everything else.

"No," I repeated. "Today has a lot of great to offer. In fact, it has already been good. You've even practiced kindness today. Remember?"

"Hurrying to the car so we wouldn't be late?" he asked.

"Maybe, but when I asked for a taste of your pumpkin chocolate chip bread, you searched your plate to find the *best* piece to give me. That was so kind. It would have been easier to give me the one you didn't want."

"That's so small though," he countered.

"No, it isn't. You put someone else ahead of yourself, giving away what you love. And it made me feel pretty special."

No act of kindness is too small. We need to give ourselves a break. Grab hold of mercy's compassion and recognize that some days (Mondays especially) are hard. And reach for a few of the many things for which to be thankful.

Together, Birdie and I started to tick things off. And it all came from sharing a bite off a paper plate. Then he got out of the car encouraged and with thoughts of goodness, of thankfulness, of kindness, and of mercy fresh in his mind.

We both did.

ALONGSIDE

KIND: Naturally

Since starting the Peace Project, I find myself more naturally nice, even though I'm really not mean or anything.

Like yesterday, a guy wouldn't move over and let me on the freeway. My first instinct was to get mad, but I stopped myself—not wanting to be that way.

Old habits die hard. But even though I've been busy and sometimes miss the chance to be kind, I'm at least cognitively aware. Which, in turn, lightens my load.

—CJ—

TKM How have you practiced?
What have you learned?

The best portion of a good man's life is his little, nameless, unremembered acts of kindness and of love.

WILLIAM WORDSWORTH

DAY 19

Words

> Maybe trust is less about God being some superhero who swoops in and saves the day just as I was about to give up. Maybe trust is more like the sigh of relief I take when I get home after a long day. Maybe it is more this assurance that I have a place where I am safe and loved, even when chaos is happening outside those doors or inside my soul.
>
> AMENA BROWN

Mercy is making me consider words used with others and with ourselves. Written, texted, spoken aloud, as well as those we say in our thoughts silently that are actually so loud. Are the words seasoned with grace—the grace that paves mercy's path?

"I'm stupid," the kid riding shotgun muttered to himself. "Just dumb. Stupid."

He had forgotten something at home, which was not a big deal. But it flung open the door to an opportunity for him to negatively self-speak.

We all do it. We lace words with judgment, shame, and guilt. We make declarations of insignificance and lack in all sorts of forms, many of which stay inside our heads, and some of which, like my morning passenger's, actually cross our lips where they can be tasted and heard, creating a major pothole in our neural pathways. Yet another return to our issue with mindsight that isn't always—okay, is rarely—20/20.

Poet and author Amena Brown shared with the *SaySomething* carpool-chat gang what she calls (and named a book after) *broken records*: recurring messages that we live with a long time.

"Now being at a point in life to be able to say, 'Are those messages good?'" she told us, "I stop. And when they're not good, I call it out, 'How long have I been holding on to that?'"

We nodded in agreement because we can all relate.

Then Amena encouraged herself and each of us to go beyond calling out, to consider lifting the needle and switching over to a new album. "What's the truth that I should be repeating versus that ugly message that's been repeating?

"We all know the Golden Rule to 'love your neighbor as yourself,'" she continued, "but we forget or have never seen an equally important part. It goes like this: The Golden Rule, *Love your neighbor*—oh, and by the way—*AND love yourself*."[1]

Why is it so hard to stop the broken records that we play on repeat? I don't know, but it's very much worth calling them out and putting on a Truth LP album to take its place, or at least to give it equal airtime. Truth that slays all the what-ifs and enoughs—as in, *are we* or *can we ever* be enough?—is the truth that we are okay, enough, loved, accepted. That we belong.

Amena continued our conversation, saying, "In the end, I do give away the secret to fixing our broken records. And here it is: we, in and of ourselves, cannot."

We all laughed at her conclusion.

"Amen," my friend Brenda said.

"That's a hard one, right?" Amena asked us.

It is hard. We can't help but fall short in our own efforts as we're so often tethered to the measuring-up-in-order-to-be-okay messages. We must look outside of ourselves to let those inside messages be informed by God's declarations over us—the eternal truth anchored in his love.

Those messages that can easily become or have already gotten stuck on repeat—the "I'm not loveable," "I'm not adequate," "I'm not enough" statements—can be paused and discarded in the face of God, the one who has already determined our worth and declared our identity.

Dare we walk away from the negative conversations? Those external and internal broken records?

In practicing thankfulness, kindness, and mercy around our house, we've been moved by the way mercy has prompted each of us to walk away from a conversation. It can be so hard to do when the topic is about someone whose actions or traits warrant a little gossipy group chat. But there's more power in choosing compassion, within healthy boundaries, and saying something true that is uplifting and kind. Or, as my grandmother always told us, "If you can't say anything nice, don't say anything."

Holding back on harsh words is a gift of kindness to the one holding back as much as the one not maligned—even when the unspoken words are true. Even when everyone is griping. Even when it feels so right to fire something up. Even when we've been wronged or offended and just need to let everyone know. Speaking negative words seems powerful and justified, but the simple, kind act of holding one's tongue is much more powerful. Not in avoidance but out of kindness—fighting for compassion and understanding.

It's so easy to judge and join in, or even start, the conversation rather than find a spot of compassion—especially with people, or even family members, who have hurt us. If the words "Oh, and another thing" are uttered, maybe stop and consider what's coming on the other side. Will they be words that build up? Or words that (though they may be true) tear down?

I love this quote from a poem by Mary Ann Pietzker: "Before you speak, let your words pass through three gates: Is it True? Is it Necessary? Is it Kind?"[2]

Others have taken her phrase and made it an acronym:

THINK before you speak (even self-speak):
Is it **T**rue?
Is it **H**elpful?
Is it **I**nspiring (building up)?
Is it **N**ecessary?
Is it **K**ind?

So as Birdie and I pulled up for the morning drop-off I turned and looked him straight on. As I saw the expression of self-doubt on his face, I thought how I would adore this kid even if we didn't share the same last name. "Listen," I said, "light bosses the dark, not the other way around. Here's some truth-light to shine on those dark thoughts."

And I dove in. "Let me tell you who you are. You're seen, you're known, and you're loved—by me and your dad and your siblings, for sure. You are kind and generous, and you work hard. You're fun and creative and you're a nice person. So hear those words. They are all true. And that's that."

I gave him a smile, then said, "Now get out." Then I kicked him out of the car with a singsongy, "I'll see you this afternoon!"

He may not be able to speak those words himself, and he may not believe me, but words of truth are light and life and they don't fall to the ground.

One thing about light is that it absolutely always bosses the dark. I watched it earlier that morning. The light shined through the trees on our dark morning walk, casting shadows to create art that could rival any hanging on museum walls. It was so beautiful and peaceful as it beamed forth through the branches bossing the dark. As it did later in the car with our words.

What is your broken record?

For my shotgun rider, negative self-talk was on continuous play that morning. He needed a new tune. New tunes come not only with an album change but also by getting to the bottom of why those messages are getting so much airtime. What is at the core?

It takes time and trust to get to the why.

ALONGSIDE

KIND: Words

I'm catching myself and what I say. We're always speaking words over others and ourselves.

The simplest act of kindness can be saying words that build up and don't tear down—for others and myself.

—AR—

TKM How have you practiced?
What have you learned?

Maybe it is more this assurance that I have a place where I am safe and loved, even when chaos is happening outside those doors or inside my soul.

AMENA BROWN

DAY 20

Getting to Why

> Lord, grant that I might not so much seek to be loved as to love.
>
> SAINT FRANCIS OF ASSISI

One of many perks that come with having a mom who lives close by is that when she was buying fall wreaths for her door, she bought one for mine as well.

I was backing out of our drive when she pulled up behind me and lightly honked. Snopes and I stopped what we were doing, begged her to come in, and enjoyed hanging the wreath with her before she was on to the next thing.

Moments matter.

I heard an interview later that day while running errands. In it, a highly accomplished and dignified actor shared about the silly phone calls he would get from his mom and the way he would roll his eyes and chide her that whatever she shared on her calls didn't matter. But he also said that he would give anything for her to be calling with such silly things today, as she had since passed away. The silly things didn't matter, but she did—so very much.

Moments *and people* matter.

Moments and people are where we have seen mercy consistently, mysteriously, powerfully usher in a lightness of being. Mercy sees to the soul. It engages humanity and offers freedom. Freedom from long-standing prisons, such as baggage from past events, hurts, relational issues, or just old habits. And if it has not provided freedom, mercy has at least prompted such prisons to be addressed or brought into the light for addressing. And we know what light does: it bosses.

Mercy also invites why into the conversation. Maybe it's only through mercy that we feel safe enough to go to why, which is where even more freedom lies.

If we're willing to go there, *why* can come to the rescue so that when feelings of unsettledness or misgiving or even of spiraling start to enter the picture, we can stop, call them out, and get to the source rather than isolate or quit.

I had an opportunity to practice why recently. While I was in carpool, a friend sent me a well-intentioned text that landed sour.

> I wanted to clarify our conversation yesterday. I didn't say anything then, but felt you may have misunderstood my efforts. Anyway, I talked with Brian about it and . . .

No need to go any further. I think it was around the word *clarify* that I started to feel unsettled, for sure at *I didn't say anything then*. By the time *you may have misunderstood* came around, you could have stuck a fork in me—I was done. My guard was up. The implication that I was off in my response to what she had said about me the day before was made clear by the *I talked with Brian*, which really hit a chord. I had to put my phone down and breathe. I felt vulnerable and judged, then judged even more by another someone outside of our conversation.

My reaction was an overreaction since her message was intended as nice.

The misgivings I felt acted like an indicator light that I should start to ask myself, *Why*? My unsettledness offered a good time to pause and take inventory of what messaging was going on in my head or what stress may have been making me sensitive. Sometimes misgivings or feelings of unsettledness are reasonable and warranted. Other times such feelings have nothing to do with what is at hand. Misgivings can stem from old emotional wounds and past happenings that we have never fully addressed. We can find ourselves wallowing in those places without realizing it.

Even reading this friend's text now makes me wonder how I ever received it so negatively.

Why did the text frustrate me? Getting to the why invited mercy for her—she was simply being kind, trying to out her own misgivings—and mercy for myself through compassion because past hurts can easily misinform today.

I really don't like people talking about things that involve me behind my back, which goes back to old emotional wounds and fears during situations where conversations concerning me were held when I wasn't there to weigh in. I never liked those feelings.

And on the day I received the text, that's what flooded my thoughts. Old hurts were weighing in on new conversations.

We may not be able to go back and change yesterday, but we do have the choice about what we do today. And choice is a powerful tool. It can either set us back, if we choose to wallow and hold tight to old hurts and ways of thinking, or it can propel us forward as we choose a different ending.

A few years ago, Dr. Dan Baker, who started Canyon Ranch, a lovely getaway spot in Arizona, wrote a book titled *What Happy People Know*. In it he talked about choice as the "father of freedom" in terms of emotional freedom. "Anyone can choose the course of their lives, but only happy people do it."[1]

And the most powerful tool in our freedom kit? Wait for it—appreciation. Yes, thankfulness.

Martha Beck, Harvard-educated life coach and author, adds that

> joyful people finish their life stories on a very different note: appreciation. Instead of going over and over what they've lost, they focus on what they've gained.[2]

She points out that a key to handling trauma is talking, calling it out, and walking through it with someone sympathetic who cares, a process that goes a long way in healing emotional wounds. "But when our cultural focus on 'the talking cure' joins forces with our natural inclination toward negativity, we can get stuck."[3]

My grandmother also told us, "Too much of a good thing goes bad fast." Which I learned almost every time I left her house. She loved to bake and made the best cookies. Just thinking about them makes my mouth water. She knew each one of her grandchildren's favorite cookies and would often send us out with a coffee tin lovingly filled to the lid with them. I remember trying my hardest to keep that lid closed, to save my cookies. But, of course, I would allow just one and save the rest. Because it's rude not to partake of a gift someone has made for you, right?

So I would eat one. And that one, in all its yummy deliciousness, would beg for another and another and another until half the can was consumed. So delicious. But soon my head would start to hurt from the sugar rush, and I would crash only miles away from her house. The funny thing is I knew exactly what would happen, yet I still did it pretty much every time.

I think about that as it applies to ruminating on painful past happenings. The talking is good. The acknowledging is good. But reliving over and over again—not so much. We can exercise our choice to acknowledge past hurt and move on, giving ourselves mercy along the way as we embrace and live through forgiveness, remembering Corrie ten Boom's friend's illustration that a bell may still ring as it slows to a stop.

For me, something more must have been at play when I got the text. And once I examined it, it wasn't rocket science.

I'm so thankful for kind and honest friends with whom I can safely talk. And that's exactly what I did. I went to a friend's house, pulled up the text, and walked through my reaction. I honestly thought I'd forgiven the sender and moved on from the bold feelings of rejection, insignificance, and apparently bitterness from a completely unrelated issue. But when the text came, some deep hurt from the past tagged along for the ride.

Questioning why the words hurt opened the door for me to get to core issues and reframe them according to thankfulness, kindness, and mercy.

The truth? Any feelings of rejection or insignificance can instantly be transformed by simple facts. I'm not alone. My dear friend is next to me, walking through emotional issues in the same way I walk with her. And even deeper and more eternally significant, God has declared acceptance and supreme significance over us, backing up words with action through Christ. Ruminating on that for a minute, ditching the negative thoughts and standing in a shower of grace-filled, abundant love and safety replaces feelings of judgment and rejection.

The narrative changes.

And the end of the story is changed from being informed by a negative road shaped by past hurt to appreciation for all I have. Genuinely.

For some, it might not end there. Deeper issues associated with trauma or illness may need deeper help. This is simply a starting point to claim the victory that has been won and to reach first for freedom rather than be imprisoned by old wounds.

Until then, Martha Beck says it so beautifully as she invites us to consider that our emotional wounds aren't nothing. "They're epic sagas that end with beauty, courage or wisdom. You don't have to feel that way immediately, but you'll get there eventually if you can find a way to honor your own story without sinking beneath it."[4]

Especially as we lean into eternal truth—the story behind the story, the greater story.

ALONGSIDE

MERCY: Conflict Resolver

The secret sauce to resolving conflict is figuring out that it is always about the person who is speaking. It's not possible for me to rewrite everything that brought the person to where they are now. Nor could anyone rewrite what brought me to where I am. So in conflict, be aware and take the opportunity to find grace. Lest we respond out of anger or frustration—where there is no-win.

The Peace Project has given me an invitation to feel differently during my day. And what a gift. I feel power in a situation—by simply being nice to a person—and it actually gives me freedom and peace. It has been a Soul30. I wasn't sure I could do it, but for thirty days I tried and the practices came to mind every day.

—CB—

TKM How have you practiced?
What have you learned?

Lord, grant that I might not so much seek to be loved as to love.

SAINT FRANCIS OF ASSISI

DAY 21

Deep Well of Grace

> Grace is not part of consciousness; it is the amount of light in our souls, not knowledge nor reason.
>
> POPE FRANCIS

When contemplating and practicing mercy and kindness, it's almost impossible to do so without grace. With all its many facets, grace warrants more attention than we tend to give it. I love the way that Saint Augustine explains it: "Grace is given not because we have done good works, but in order that we may be able to do them."[1] It's as if willingness is the combustion needed to start mercy's engine and grace is the fuel to put motion into mercy's acts of compassion and forgiveness.

It's funny how quick we are to accept, or even expect, grace. Yet we're equally as fast to skirt extending it and tick through reasons substantiating why we shouldn't give it out.

On our thirty-day journey, I kept track of the ways I practiced thankfulness, kindness, and mercy in the notes section of my phone. Writing it all down daily held me accountable, not in some shaming sort of way since I wanted to do it, but in a way that allowed me to go back and remember. So after twenty days of the experiment had passed, I did a "grace" search to see if it had shown up anywhere in my notes. Of the twenty days, twelve documented grace.

Grace is almost always next to compassion. I think that's because it comes when we stop long enough to see that there is more to the story. In fact, I didn't have to look very far. Just the other day, I was stopped in my tracks.

"But I said you would go," I slightly bossed the kid whose feet were dragging at the thought of an event he didn't want to attend.

"I can't," Birdie replied.

"You can and will," I responded, not wanting to back out on a commitment. Barton raised her eyebrows and shook her head at me as a little message-reminder that I heard loud and clear. Her brother had lived a hard week. A few mean things had come his way, making him not ready to enter into a free-for-all gathering of teenage boys.

"You know," I said, "you don't need to go. I have something I'd love for you to help me with tonight. I'll let them know there was a mix-up." It wasn't a lie. Some mixed up things, indeed, needed unmixing.

The color almost instantly came back into his face, and he breathed a little easier. He would have gone had I insisted, and he would have done so with his head held high. But the relief of getting a break from stressful interaction infused life into his day. I didn't realize the stress level was so high.

Showing mercy to my son invited compassion and grace into the situation. Certain times in life and certain circumstances can fire up stress. And stress is real. As is the amazing resilience woven within people who may still need grace. An extra measure of compassion can go a long way. As does a redirect in the form of acts that can help remind us of the greater story. Which is how I planned to use Birdie's help.

We walked our block, and he helped me put little sacks of muffins on doorsteps, invitations for a coffee gathering. I cherished the help from my son. Just the time spent walking outside, being needed and doing something for others, put meat on the bones of the talk we had while doing it.

Grace, though arguably one of the most amazing aspects of humanity, can be a complicated topic. Religious circles run to it, then often instantly run from it since the freedom it invites is too good to be true in a world tethered to performance.

Author and theologian Frederick Buechner beautifully and thoughtfully opines,

> After centuries of handling and mishandling, most religious words have become so shopworn nobody's much interested anymore. Not so with grace. . . .
>
> Grace is something you can never get but only be given. There's no way to earn it or deserve it or bring it about any more than you can deserve the taste of raspberries and cream or earn good looks or bring about your own birth.
>
> A good sleep is grace and so are good dreams. Most tears are grace. . . . Somebody loving you is grace. Loving somebody is grace.[2]

His words bring to mind my father-in-law, who recently visited our house. While here, he was intent on getting each of the kids' personal email addresses. He sends the most wonderful correspondence—usually to his grown kids (and lucky spouses), but up until recently, he has been sending them to our kids through me. I used to fight not to read his words before forwarding them on. Now that he can go directly to their inboxes, I'll miss that.

I'm thankful for the legacy he's leaving through his emails, especially those he sent during some of the challenging years when I think he felt a bit lonely.

Like most people, his life has taken a few detour twists that he just didn't imagine for himself when serving alongside his bride with an indigenous tribe on a tributary of the Amazon River for fifty years. He and my mother-in-law were forced into retirement around their fiftieth wedding anniversary when Alzheimer's entered the picture.

Before she died, we watched him move from serving the Ese Eja tribe to serving her with grace.

His emails offered a peek into grace lived out—like this note he sent after my mother-in-law had a hip replacement.

> It is good to have the surgery completed. The doctor removed the staples on Thursday. He showed us the X-ray and the new ball and post in the femur looks good. She cannot bear weight yet, but we're hoping that will come at least to some measure. Wouldn't it be nice if other problems could be fixed by a nice neat surgery? She continues quite tired, eyes half closed, and it's hard to get her to say a few words.
>
> She is now in the rehab section at the "Convalescent Center" and with some coaching from the therapist, I am learning the feeding technique. It is a good session if she can feed herself a little. Most of the time she requires much help. Remember when we tried to feed our kids and how happy we were when they managed to get a little into their mouths? Getting her fingers around the spoon, down to the plate, scooping up a bit, and moving it to her mouth is the start. Then I encourage her on, "Chew, sweetheart. Swallow, sweetheart" as the therapist tells me to check her mouth to see if she is holding some off to the side, then suggests, "If you touch her throat, she may get the idea." We encourage her on as we see her throat move, and we can proceed to one more bite. She needs to take nourishment by mouth. I haven't been too successful the last two evenings. The nurse did say she ate better at noon.
>
> I think of the hundreds of meals she had prepared and so joyfully served to us and so many who visited. I am thankful (most of the time) that I can help her now in these small ways. Suffering always tests our trust in God's love and sovereignty and has a sanctifying effect in our lives.

His actions are a picture of grace extended through selfless service. Grace for which his wife could do nothing, literally nothing, in return. Often she was unaware of days or the people around her, yet grace permeated their relationship through love. It's interesting to consider that neither could have engaged with grace without it willfully being given. Then grace had to be received in order to be experienced. I could probably use a little lesson from my mother-in-law on receiving grace.

Mercy and grace go hand in hand. Though they differ, they operate in the same space and affect our brains in a similar fashion. We know that mercy involves compassion and grace.

Frederick Buechner concludes:

> The grace of God means something like: "Here is your life. You might never have been, but you *are*, because the party wouldn't have been complete without you. Here is the world. Beautiful and terrible things will happen. Don't be afraid. I am with you. Nothing can ever separate us. It's for you I created the universe. I love you."
>
> There's only one catch. Like any other gift, the gift of grace can be yours only if you'll reach out and take it.
>
> Maybe being able to reach out and take it is a gift too.[3]

May we be inspired as we continue our journey of practicing thankfulness, kindness, and mercy to extend grace and accept it too. Because grace is a gift best experienced by giving it and accepting it from someone else.

ALONGSIDE

KINDNESS AND MERCY: Wonder Twins

I now find myself seeing people I would normally have looked through. I've found myself noticing and wondering if they need help and if there's a way I can offer it.

My kids are noticing too.

Gratitude and kindness have opened our eyes to look out beyond ourselves and actually have very real compassion when we normally would have gone on with our day and missed out.

It's funny, I thought I would have to brainstorm on ways to be kind. Maybe even come up with a big list. I've been surprised that I never have needed to look. Things have popped up every day without me even asking, which has taken something like acts of kindness from being a task to being a spiritual journey.

Combining kindness with mercy takes the works aspect out. Making them an overflow instead.

—MJ—

TKM How have you practiced?
What have you learned?

Grace is not part of consciousness; it is the amount of light in our souls, not knowledge nor reason.

POPE FRANCIS

DAY 22

Because/Then Statements

> Scales always lie. They don't make a scale that ever told the truth about value, about worth, about significance.
>
> ANN VOSKAMP

"Hey." I turned back to face one of the boys as he hopped out of our car.

Apparently, we *are* in the car most of the time. I know a day is coming soon when that won't be the case. Or, at least, I think that day is coming. What I know for sure is the fact that I will miss the car days. The time spent just sitting with my people.

"I want you to know that I loved how you stopped in the middle of your day yesterday to see if you could get your sister a coffee on your way home," I told him. "Sweet that you had her on your mind and that you would act on it."

"It was nothing." He shook his head.

"No, it was far from nothing." I tried to reframe his action for him. This is my one who thinks very few nice things about himself. "It was nice. You think kindness and do it. I really like that about you."

"Okay," he said as he got out.

I think I saw a smile.

Regardless, a little truth crossed his ears.

Birdie, who was still sitting next to me, added, "You know, I've gone in and gotten her a coffee too."

I laughed. He has. He's a kind soul.

We stopped for movie popcorn on our way home, which we sometimes splurge and do. There's a theater close to one of the schools, and, really, what is better than fresh movie popcorn? Especially if you have some M&Ms to sprinkle in it. (Delicious.) As we pulled up, I gave Birdie money to run in, and I told him to keep the change. Just to make his day.

This kid is not only kind; he loves people. He gets to know folks wherever he goes, making friends along the way—including the staff in the movie theater. Anthony, a retired teacher, happened to be on deck manning the concessions counter that afternoon. Birdie ran in, ordered a medium popcorn, chatted with Anthony a bit, handed him the money, then headed back to the car.

"Who was working today?" I asked as I grabbed a handful of popcorn. I feel like I know the theater employees through Birdie.

"Anthony," he said. "He's doing great. He's just so nice and does such a good job. I told him to keep the change."

"That's sweet," I said, then I remembered that I had told Birdie whatever was left was *his*.

Had he forgotten? "Honey, that money was yours to keep."

"I know," he chirped. "I was so excited you said I could have it. I even thought about a game I've been wanting and how it would help me with what I've already saved. And as happy as it made me to think about what I could get, I watched Anthony fill my sack with popcorn and thought it could make him as happy as it could make me. So I told him it was his."

"It was a twenty," I said. I really had splurged that day. I thought I would surprise my son with something super nice.

"A twenty-dollar bill?" He was wide-eyed. "I didn't look. I just said keep it." Then again, "A twenty?" He glanced over at me in a bit of disbelief. "Why would you say to keep the change from a twenty?"

"I just wanted you to have it."

"Wow. Thank you." He smiled—sort of letting it sink in. Honestly, it wasn't that big of a deal. Who knew it would mean so much?

"Well," he said as he thought about it all, "I'm happy Anthony has it. He's so kind to me and to others. Always. And kindness makes everyone feel good, even though this time it wasn't free." He laughed.

We've pointed out on several occasions that kindness is free, so I guess Birdie thought, *Why not freely give it?*

"It's weird how the person being kind feels SO great," he continued. "*And* how the person receiving it feels the same way. And it makes you feel good for a while. My keep-the-change to him made me feel as great as it probably made him feel. Maybe better. So that keep-the-change has spread a lot of good feelings."

He's right. And he is kind like his brother.

Funny how, at the surface, doubt stands ready to make us question ourselves. Birdie's *You know, I go in and get her a coffee too* was his effort to calm some doubt. Self-doubt entertains questions that arise when we let what someone else is doing somehow inform our significance, our worth, and our identity. As if someone else's actions—our measurement next to them as an up or down—carry the determining factor for us on any given day or experience.

Why do we do that to ourselves? Are we only as good or lacking as our last act? Do we let the lacking, or even perception of lacking, take ground in our thoughts, leaving us flailing in the wind?

At that point we find ourselves at the mercy of life's grand if/then statement: *If* you do or have this, *then* you're okay. If you don't, then you're not. It's a brutal economy that rarely invites thriving since the other side of life's if/then statement is ever changing, always elusive.

But a peek behind the greater story's curtain reveals that life's if/then statements are the furthest thing from what waits for us in the wings. Grabbing eternal-perspective lenses brings into focus a much more powerful and solid equation. With them we can see that a because/then statement put into place by the story's Creator answers doubt.

It goes a little something like this:

> Because God says you're steadfastly loved,[1] then you can live free from performance pressures.
>
> Because God says you're "honored in [his] sight,"[2] then you can let go of the need to prove yourself.
>
> Because God provides perfect provision,[3] then you can lean in to the certainty of his sustenance.
>
> Because God is faithful[4] (and cannot be unfaithful, as it would be counter to his character), then you can rest.
>
> Because God bestows his strength upon you,[5] then you can ditch striving.
>
> Because God says you are known ("I have called you by name; you are mine"), then you can operate out of the fullness of belonging.[6]

The list goes on and on. It's just so hard to grasp or believe since God's because/then economy operates so differently than most of what we see and know. And God's because/then statements are intimate, spoken to us collectively as well as exclusively. For each person has been created in his image with exclusive and unique purpose, plans, and giftedness prepared in advance for us.

I looked over at my *You know, I go in and get her a coffee too* kid and said, "Hey—you know on the getting your sister coffee thing we talked about earlier?"

"Yes," he said, munching on the popcorn. I'm sure he was wondering why I was going back to that.

"What your brother is doing has no bearing on you," I told him. "I know you get her coffee. I see and I love the kindness in your heart and your actions. You have a lane just like he does. Appreciate and be inspired by each other, alongside. Forget against."

"Yeah maybe," he replied. I can't believe he listens to me. I zone myself out sometimes. But I could tell he was listening since he proceeded to teach me something. "I think God gives us opportunities like this one to remind us that trying to keep up or get ahead makes us feel terrible. But kindness always feels good." He paused. "I'm glad for that twenty dollars."

He ate a few more handfuls of popcorn, then with his mouth full, he added with a smirk, "Well, unless I'm doing something kind to *look* good."

Well—yes.

I love thinking through things with him. "Never forget," I couldn't help but add, "God has declared you okay."

God's because/then statements seal our significance today and forever. Operating out of that truth invites kindness and mercy to transform.

TKM How have you practiced?
What have you learned?

____

____

____

____

____

____

Scales always lie. They don't make a scale that ever told the truth about value, about worth, about significance.

ANN VOSKAMP

DAY 23

Settled Significance

> Lord, when I feel that what I'm doing is insignificant and unimportant, help me to remember that everything I do is significant and important in your eyes, because you love me and you put me here, and no one else can do what I am doing in exactly the way I do it.
>
> BRENNAN MANNING

"You're a giver," I told my friend Charlotte the other day.

I'm not sure she even realizes the impact she has since most of her giving is silent. She saw our coffee need at weekly gatherings in my home and was on it. She called a local coffeehouse and set up a standing order so that I wouldn't have that on my plate every Tuesday morning. She just showed up—carafe filled with fresh hot coffee, a stack of to-go cups, creamer, and sweeteners in hand—sweetly smiling, expecting nothing in return.

Yes. She's a giver.

When our friend Jen lost her battle with cancer, leaving behind people she loved, a husband of less than ten years and a four-year-old son, Charlotte quietly slipped into their home where Jen had spent her last days. Not wanting Jen's husband to handle one item from the final weeks, Charlotte cleaned, washed, straightened, and transformed the room back to all its original loveliness as its loveliest person was no longer there. Fighting her own tears and loss, she quietly served. Because that's what she does.

Definitely a giver.

"I don't think so," Charlotte replied to my compliment. "I can kind of get irritated with my family."

Our friend Bev happened to be standing next to us, and she weighed in with a load of honesty. "It's probably because the people next to you are takers."

The comment stopped us all in our tracks. She wasn't trying to be mean or rude; she was simply stating a fact. Bev knows Charlotte is a giver too.

"Yup," she continued. "It's true in general but especially so in families. People fall into roles. Takers and givers. The givers keep giving, often to their detriment. The takers tend to have no clue they're taking. They just do."

"I've lived it today," she said. "I stepped up to help a family that just can't see the needs of their sister, my friend, who is a giver. And she can't express her need without being overwhelmed by feelings of guilt. So everyone is stagnant. It's what we as people do. Fall into roles and get stuck. Then we walk around with all sorts of baggage and heavy thoughts. It's textbook."

It cracked me up how matter-of-fact Bev said what she had to say. I think it was on her mind since she had arrived late to our Tuesday morning study because she was helping the friend she was telling us about.

Welcome to chaos that naturally occurs inside and outside ourselves.

We assume roles—in our families and in our everyday lives. Some that we realize, many that fall into business as usual, most that we aren't aware of until we're made aware.

In *Psychology Today,* authors Linda and Charlie Bloom share an example:

> The over-functioning husband with the under-functioning wife is only one of an array of patterns imported from our original families that can become a destructive force. . . . The adult who had been the clown in his family of origin can drive his wife [or friends] nuts making jokes every time she brings up a serious subject she wants to discuss. . . . Those who were peacemakers in their original family may become anger-phobic and attempt to smooth out differences before a healthy interchange can take place.
>
> . . . The huge advantage of bringing the roles we played as children up to conscious mind is that we then can see more clearly that as adults, we have maturity, power and the sophistication to make wiser choices.[1]

In life, we adopt certain standards or molds as they relate to being a man, woman, child, young adult, parent, or fill in the blank. We fall in line with our roles, often roles determined by our environment or expectations, and don't think twice about their effect on us. We don't notice them until someone bucks the system. At which point, mercy can come in and help us see that the system doesn't own us.

Bev had willingly entered her friend's chaos to help. She did it with honest mercy, understanding the person involved but never beholden to her chaos.

She told us more about the story. "I gently explained to my friend what I see at the core of the frustrations with her family, as well as herself, is the victim-status in her own mind. I'm not sure she can hear it yet. But she's my friend—so I'll keep at it."

"I think I do some of that," Charlotte replied. "The other day we were traveling, and I offered to hold a coat, which I then found myself doing for hours. I had planned to just hold it while my adult kid put his bags overhead. But I held the coat the whole flight. Then through the airport and car ride to our destination. And to myself, I said to my son—*Do you see me holding your coat? Do I look like a coatrack?* Then I kind of got frustrated, and—"

"I bet you felt totally insignificant, maybe a little resentful—then probably passive-aggressive," Bev interjected. She's actually a licensed professional with an emphasis on conflict management, so she gets below the surface fast. She's a great friend to have.

Knowing Charlotte's sweet family, I added, "And I bet they don't even know. Even though to you, it probably feels like you're their servant."

"Yes." Charlotte nodded.

"Yup—that's how it goes," Bev said. "Givers and takers—people assume their roles."

"But if we go to truth," I said, thinking out loud, "and can grasp that our significance is settled, there is no need at all to feel like a welcome mat. Because we're not. You're not." I looked over at Charlotte and thought how we tend to sell ourselves short. Seriously, if we can get the part about our significance determined—like it's a done deal—we can ditch the walked-on or unseen feelings that pop up and try to take over something as good as being nice by helping with a coat.

"So you hold the coat," Bev gently encouraged, "and the minute you start feeling taken for granted—call it out in your mind. The idea of insignificance is completely unfounded. In fact, nothing is further from the truth."

"Right." I nodded in agreement. "It goes back to God's because/then declarations. Because your significance is settled: you are seen, known, and loved. Then you can hold the coat just to be kind and pass it back with no hard feelings."

"Yes." Bev nodded.

"Settled significance . . . ," Charlotte said slowly, chewing on the words as if to digest them.

I keep learning about the power of operating from worth, identity, and settled significance as determined by God. I think it is the key to kindness and mercy. And thankfulness is the on-ramp to get there.

"Gosh—without our significance settled, kindness and mercy can go all funky fast," Charlotte added. "But with it, there's nothing more beautiful."

TKM How have you practiced?
What have you learned?

Lord, when I feel that what I'm doing is insignificant and unimportant, help me to remember that everything I do is significant and important in your eyes, because you love me and you put me here, and no one else can do what I am doing in exactly the way I do it.

BRENNAN MANNING

DAY 24

Alongside, Not Against

> Start by doing what's necessary; then do what's possible; and suddenly you are doing the impossible.
>
> SAINT FRANCIS OF ASSISI

Weeks often seem to fly by. I look up and it's Friday before I know it. Whatever I needed to get done on Monday is usually still undone by the end of the week. Phone calls I thought I would return the minute after listening to a message remain unreturned. Somehow the day ends almost before it starts. Multiple texts I started, then got distracted from, have moved down the queue to the Land of the Lost—until the very kind person texts me back and I see my start/stop debacle, reminding me of all the open loops.

My goodness. I feel for anyone who crosses the wake of my chaos.

"I need to write down what I need to get done," I thought out loud as Snopes and I sat together in the car. "Maybe if I make a list I'll actually remember to do these things that *must* be done. Today."

"Good idea," she encouraged. "I think it would take a lot of stress out of your life. They make a huge difference in mine."

Inspired, I pulled out a cute card from my console and started to write.

Discount Tire
Visa/Passport place
Call Lisa
Salsa stuff/store
Tuesday Morning

"You've got to add something fun. Just to check it off," she told me. "Like 'Lunch.'"

"Great idea." I added *Lunch.*

So that's where we started.

"I don't usually make lists," I told her. "Probably because I lose them within minutes of making them. Then I think I'll remember. But I don't until the end of the week, and I wonder how I got nothing done."

"I make lists all the time," she said. "And I check things off. In fact, if I need to get things done in a class, I don't write *Math*—I go for specifics. A line for each thing, like *Read pages thirty through thirty-five; Do problems one through eight; Study vectors* or whatever there is. It feels good to check things off. Productivity inspires productivity."

Her words sounded like something you'd read on an inspirational cat poster at the local discount store. But what she suggested was a great idea. So, with her help, I started with my tiny list for the day, determined to get it done.

Lunch. *Check.* I called Lisa while driving to the visa/passport place. *Check.* Then the distractions started.

Honestly, in my wearer-of-many-hats role, curveballs come with the territory. Maybe I should put those on the list and check *them* off.

Curveballs. *Check.*

A couple of emails in need of instant attention popped up and were handled easily enough while sitting in the carpool line. (Next list, I'm adding carpool! *Easy check.*) I tried to buy stuff to make salsa on the way home from two detours after picking up Birdie, but the store was out of jalapeños. And on it went. I stopped at Tuesday Morning but couldn't find what we needed, though I did find something else. And I still had to return to the visa/passport office since that, too, fell short.

The afternoon continued to fly by, and I had already forgotten about Discount Tire until I looked at my list.

I called Snopes, who I had dropped at home with Birdie, "Thank you SO much for encouraging me to make a list! I would have forgotten to go to Discount Tire *again*—and that tire has to be fixed today. Thank you!"

Together. Alongside. It's what makes life so good.

Life is better when lived alongside rather than when we live against or try to live up to something. Alongside invites meeting each other where we are. Sharing tips, admitting struggles, getting over hurdles, picking each other up, reminding, and reminding again. Alongside calms emotional waters and invites normal. It helps us see each other as regular people, living the ups, downs, forgetfulness, and successes of any given day. Alongside commiserates when things go wrong and keeps us putting one foot in front of the other. Alongside tills the ground and fertilizes the practice of getting our eyes off ourselves as it permeates kindness.

I'm thankful that Snopes encouraged and helped me with my list as she walked alongside me through the checks and the fails that day. She is kind. And I'm thankful that she met me where I was, offering the terrific suggestion to put fun and easy things on the list, simply to check them off. Each time I looked at the list, I got to see *Lunch* and be reminded of her and the fun time we had together, as well as the productive things I had already checked off the list.

And I was SO thankful for the Discount Tire reminder.

Briefly home from carpool and our surprise diversions, I grabbed the keys to the flat-tired car and a bike pump to put just enough air in the tire to get there. I looked up and there was Snopes, standing ready to pump with me. For ten minutes we took turns pumping up the tire, laughing at the entire situation and what our neighbors must have been thinking as we tried to pump while holding Mitty, who just couldn't weather watching us through the window. Of course, he barked at every passerby, making our pumping all the more challenging. The entertainment we provide to our block is endless, I'm sure.

As if they weren't already scratching their heads at us, minutes before airing up our car tire with the bike pump, I was on the ground trying, without success, to duct-tape the same car's front spoiler that was hanging down for some reason. Keeping it real, as usual.

With the tire at a reasonable pressure and the spoiler sporting my duct-tape fix, I headed out and joined the Friday afternoon traffic. I got there and Johnny-on-the-spot Fred noticed the nail in the back tire, set me up to get some much-needed new front tires and a rotation so the car was all good to go. Before sending it to the technicians, Fred kindly received a small curveball from me.

"Can I ask you one slightly weird thing?" I began.

"Of course," he said.

"So, the front spoiler thing on the car is a bit shredded and hanging down. I'm not really sure what happened, but I don't want to fix it right now. I mean, why is it there in the first place? Really what does it even do?"

Does it have a purpose? I didn't know. Yes, I was sure it did, but I just didn't have time to figure it out. The one thing I did have, I pulled from my bag.

Duct tape.

I pointed to the garage. "While you have the car up on the lift, would your technician be able to tape it up?"

I showed Fred the huge gray roll.

Wide-eyed and almost speechless, he nodded. "Yes . . . We can absolutely do that."

"Just use as much as you need and tape it all up to the bottom of the car." I smiled, nodding to myself in an effort to convince him to convince me that it would work.

What could he do but agree? "Okay—should work."

Fred didn't balk. He entered my chaos with faith that the quick fix would work. Walking alongside me without judgment, reaching for hope. Because he for sure has used duct-tape fixes to get through minor scrapes in his life too. We do what we can do.

I left the car behind as Snopes picked me up on the way to a store we hoped would have our salsa ingredients. It did. Then we grabbed Fury from swim practice and headed again for home to drop him off and get dinner started for guests who would arrive in a little over an hour . As we drove, I caught a glimpse of my list and realized that I had remembered everything. Even though some items still had to be revisited, I checked them off.

Snopes drove me back to Discount Tire and waited to be sure the car was ready. Fred saw me walk in the door, smile-waved, and started thumbing through the clear plastic folders in front of him to find mine. I cracked up as he pulled it out. Not only were the receipt and my keys in the folder but that big roll of duct tape sat loud and proud at the bottom of the pile. Hilarious.

"Did it work?" I asked excitedly.

Fred was quiet. "Oh my goodness," he replied, "I kind of got distracted with the people who came in after you and completely forgot to ask the guys to look at it."

This time I got to walk alongside him. "Oh my gosh, I do the same thing. You've got so many moving parts around here. I can't imagine how you keep it all straight. And my ask was random, for sure." That was an understatement. "Is there any way they could still try?" I asked with a slight shrug and a hopeful smile. At this point, I was committed.

"Yes!" he confidently offered. "I have an open bay and the keys. Let me just go back and let them know."

Fred headed out to the garage, and I sat down. Who cares that our shredded spoiler and duct-tape fix would now be on display for all to see? So what if people were watching?

After a quick minute, Fred was back with a big smile on his face.

"It's done!" he exclaimed.

"Really?"

"Yeah." He laughed. "When I came up with the folder and started to explain, the tech was like—'I already did it.' And I asked, 'Did what?' And he pretty much duhhed me saying it was obvious—duct tape, hanging spoiler. I got it."

"That is so funny." I shook my head.

Together. All of us.

The kindness, the mercy, the thankfulness. Permeating every aspect of an afternoon. I'm so glad that practicing these things daily has opened my eyes to their power and presence everywhere, even at Discount Tire on a busy Friday afternoon. No judgment, just togetherness. Human beings, strangers who don't know each other, compassionately living life alongside.

ALONGSIDE

KINDNESS: Identity

During this process I've realized that I've been making productivity my god—I think I've made my kids' *doing* things what matters most. I think I value productivity over being kind to my kids.

Thankfulness, kindness, and mercy have opened my eyes to what apparently matters most to me. I can so easily get frustrated if they're not being productive.

And I sure let them know.

Maybe getting to why I value productivity so greatly can help me be able to be nicer to them. I tell myself that I want them to be productive so they won't be lazy. But I think I actually buy into the idea that if they're doing something productive all the time, they will be okay.

Productive is a good thing to be, unless I've decided that I'm okay—or my kids are okay—only if they're productive. I would never have imagined getting through an issue like this by practicing kindness, thankfulness, and mercy. Being set free from an idol like productivity—though not bad in and of itself—has invited peace.

—AS—

TKM How have you practiced?
What have you learned?

Start by doing what's necessary; then do what's possible;
and suddenly you are doing the impossible.

SAINT FRANCIS OF ASSISI

DAY 25

Judgment and Mercy

> Many that live deserve death. And some that die deserve life. Can you give it to them? Then do not be too eager to deal out death in judgement. For even the very wise cannot see all ends.
>
> J. R. R. TOLKIEN

We had just gotten home from a wedding in the Texas Hill Country. Loveliness filled the entire day—from the picturesque views (we almost got in an accident while driving the winding roads, pointing out the cows, deer, and stunning vistas) to family and friends to the couple themselves. Their love for and commitment to each other and to the calling in their lives makes me smile even now. I may have cried a few times. It was like beauty had been packaged, tied with a bow, and sweetly divvied out to each of us, perfectly portioned for what we could handle.

A wedding. The coming together of people to join their lives forever is the epitome of alongside, warming the hearts of all in attendance. I think it's the way a wedding embodies belonging that makes it so attractive, especially in the newest and freshest moments where hope and love find fertilized ground in which to grow.

But sometimes at these types of gatherings, whether they involve longtime friends and family or strangers, there may be the tiniest hints of judgment lying around in the background.

"Judgment makes you feel rotten," Snopes said to me. She had been standing next to me while chatting with friends when one brought up another friend whose kid had made their college sports team. Genuine good-for-thems were said, then one of the friends added, "It's great and all, but really, is that the right thing to do? I mean, they have already spent upwards of one hundred thousand dollars over the years on teams, equipment, tournaments. And it's a private college without a scholarship. They're just throwing money away."

Snopes heard the conversation and was confused.

"Why not just be happy for them?" She shrugged as she asked me later. "Judgment can be so harsh."

At first, I had no response to the comment. I couldn't understand why anyone would care, especially as making a collegiate team is a terrific achievement. I was surprised at the judgment. The family wasn't at the wedding, just old friends whose name came up amid "Have you heard from so-and-so?" while catching up. So the assessment seemed unnecessary at best.

Their comment instantly made the people involved in the conversation nervous, likely inviting everyone to wonder what is said about their decisions and choices when they aren't around. Judging others, people judging us, us judging us, us perceiving others judging us—so many iterations can make things complicated.

Rather than joining in on judgment or checking out of the conversation, we can reach for mercy that bestows compassion upon all involved. If someone is commenting on a topic like this with disdain, it's highly likely they or someone they love has been hurt or has been faced with unmet expectations or maybe even unspoken financial difficulties. Who knows? But firing out more judgment does not help resolve things. What does help is providing a kind word to quench gossipy judgment's flames and offering a simple redirect.

At a mass celebrated in the chapel of the Casa Santa Marta in March 2019, Pope Francis encouraged getting in the habit of being merciful. The first strategy of which involves not judging.

> It is a habit that gets mixed up in our life even without us realizing it. Always! Even by beginning a conversation: "Did you see what he did?" Judgement of others. Let us think about how many times each day we judge. All of us.[1]

He continued by encouraging everyone "to learn the wisdom of generosity, the main way to overcome 'gossiping.' When we gossip about others, he said, 'we are continually judging, continually condemning, and hardly forgiving.'"[2]

Generosity is centered on giving rather than taking, which is what judging does. Judging not only takes from the person who is judged but also from the person who is judging.

"I was thinking about it after we left. Wondering why it's so gross," I shared with Snopes.

It seems that people tend to judge when they need to be right or when they're sensitive about something. I think judgment is like justification for doing or acting a certain way in our own lives. And we tend to involve others in the judging in order to further justify our actions, especially if there is any uncertainty that can be easily remedied by people joining in.

"It makes me think about Jesus admonishing people to not judge others—lest we be judged," Snopes offered. "I have always found that a bit scary."

"That can seem scary."

"I mean how do you stop judging?" she asked. "I've imagined God looking down on us judging, grieving then carrying out his justice with a little smiting. Kind of always watching for a misstep. Being disappointed. You know, stuff like that."

"Yes, but how does that fit within the fact that God loves us and we have been made whole and right—period?" It's a tough topic. "So," I added, hoping to find some solid ground, "maybe what he's telling us is 'don't judge' because when we do, we cannot help but judge ourselves. It seems the act itself stems from our need to be right or better or something along those lines. Which puts our eyes back on us."

Mercy invites freedom from the need to make ourselves okay by judging others. Mercy activates compassion and forgiveness, rather than a pointing finger or well-intentioned indictment—probably mostly for ourselves—so that we know we don't have to get ahead or put someone down for our path to be fine.

Victor Frankl, an Austrian neurologist and Holocaust survivor, offers insight in his book *Man's Search for Meaning*:

> We who lived in concentration camps can remember the men who walked through the huts comforting others, giving away their last piece of bread. They may have been few in number, but they offer sufficient proof that everything can be taken from a man but one thing: the last of the human freedoms—to choose one's attitude in any given set of circumstances, to choose one's own way.[3]

We get to choose to be a victim of judgment (whether we're dishing it out or it is thrust upon us) or to be a victor over it and bring dignity to the conversation and to the people involved.

But we may also need to address resentment and bitterness in order to get there.

ALONGSIDE

MERCY: Compassion and Innermost Freedom

In practicing mercy, we get to see the power of it so that we might be able to see mercy in another area of our life that we didn't know it could be.

This is opening up things in my life I didn't even know needed to be opened or could be opened. Crusty old stuff we might not know is there has been holding us hostage.

And the freedom is almost too good to be true. Is mercy so powerful that it's able to inform and redeem old, old, old pattern wounds? I want the kind of compassion that leads to mercy in places where I have been hostage to feelings of resentment or anger or bitterness.

I now know it's possible.

—CB—

TKM How have you practiced?
What have you learned?

Many that live deserve death. And some that die deserve life. Can you give it to them? Then do not be too eager to deal out death in judgement. For even the very wise cannot see all ends.

J. R. R. TOLKIEN

DAY 26

Magical Mercy

> Compassion is the keen awareness of the interdependence of all things.
>
> THOMAS MERTON

One of the greatest things about doing this journey with friends has been how open everyone has been to share. Not only does the openness invite *me toos* and gut checks but it also proves that practicing thankfulness, kindness, and mercy genuinely offers peace.

We had a really great conversation the last time we met to reflect on our Soul30 challenge together.

"I feel like I've been doing acts of kindness for years through volunteering and being mindful of people's needs." Leslie opened up the conversation. She is so generous with her time. "But what I'm realizing through this little Soul30 exercise is that I'm not sure I have the same happy heart with kindness toward those closest to me. I catch myself after doing something for someone in my family, realizing that I'm doing it with an ugliness rather than genuine kindness."

Her words were raw and real.

"It doesn't feel good," she continued. "And I want to get to the bottom of it. I want to focus on it and try to get to what's going on within me. You know, why I feel bad. Trying to be aware, to understand the pain so I can get to grace and hopefully forgive myself or them or something in my chaos." She sighed. "I want to know why I'm resentful."

I think we were all humbled by her honesty. She had just invited raw authenticity into the conversation.

"I have felt the same way," Jo echoed, laughing. "This morning! I was making breakfast for my husband, and honestly, I was mad. For the gazillionth time, he left his clothes on the bathroom floor for someone to pick up after him. We all know that someone is me. So I got mad on the inside—then carried it with me to breakfast where I had less than a happy heart getting things for anyone." She paused, then added, "Just remembering it makes me sick to my stomach. There was nothing happy in my doing for others. And you're right—it was so much more like ugliness than kindness."

"Ugliness rather than kindness." We've all been there. The act itself may be kind, but the heart behind it—not so much.

If we can get to the core of why something makes us resentful or angry, maybe we can let it go. It probably boils down to our feeling used or overlooked or insignificant, which pretty much is the victim status that we've already outed as unnecessary, considering our worth and identity according to God.

"You know what I think is the opposite of victim?" asked Jo. "Compassion. Maybe starting with compassion for ourselves. Admitting that our feelings are understandable. Then reaching for settled significance where full-blown mercy can grow from the place where we see each other as human beings rather than adversaries or whatever."

"That is so good." I looked around, and it seemed like everyone was letting Jo's words sink in.

"I think if we call out the victim aspect and get to the why behind what makes us mad or resentful," Bev wisely added, "we will probably find some bitterness in need of handling and healing."

And so we landed on a discussion of bitterness, which is such a terrific topic to bring out of the shadows together. Because with bitterness comes the topic of boundaries since it usually involves people and hurt that needs to be contained.

In our society, we tend to deal with bitterness by putting up boundaries for our own protection. Boundaries are important and absolutely healthy. But sometimes a small problem can arise with the boundaries we've set for ourselves. If we're on constant alert in managing our boundaries, we're basically thinking about them all the time. Which means we're thinking about ourselves all the time, as if our management or mismanagement of boundaries is our protection.

"But what if we lead with God?" I offered.

"What do you mean?" Leslie asked. "Really, I want to know."

"Okay, so thinking out loud here. What if we allow God to be our shield and contender, which, by the way, he says he is. Then, instead of feeling unseen or walked over, anchored in our settled identity, our connection with bitterness is changed."

Charlotte nodded. "Leading with settled significance."

"For me this morning," Jo offered, "it was the way I was spoken to. It made me feel terrible."

"Rightfully so," Bev told her. "Some of it goes back to the roles we slide into." Then Bev offered gentle wisdom. "So much of our bitterness stems from natural assumption. Manipulation can play a role too. But still, if we've gone to our why and had that reframed by settled significance, maybe that's where we can find compassion as we venture into the why of others."

"You know," Jo added, "selfishly, or maybe more self-protectively, sometimes I don't want to be genuinely kind or extend mercy since I've felt like I've been walked over. But really, those words couldn't be further from the eternal reality."

She was right. Because whatever is dished on us that would prompt misgivings or resentment toward people is handled at the grandest level when we lean into our settled significance, our worth, and our identity. Handing our emotions over to bitterness is what makes us feel powerless. Handing our emotions over to God invites freedom where bitterness has no place.

"Maybe that's why mercy is so powerful," Leslie said.

What a conversation.

My friend Shelley stopped me on the way out. "Thanks for this," she said sweetly.

"Thank *you*," I said back. I'm thinking I'm the one who has scored. These women, the honesty. Such great stuff.

"I've realized that I have a lot of bitterness in my heart for ex-coworkers who have thrown me under the bus," Shelley told me. "They used me as a scapegoat for something they did.

"Yesterday," she continued, "I was with a client when one of those ex-coworkers had to help me. And with my significance settled thanks to legitimate practicing these last few weeks, I could genuinely lead with mercy and compassion. Afterword, I even hugged that person, told him thank you, and wished him a good day. It was like letting it go.

"And as I journaled for Soul30 at the end of the day, I sailed through gratitude and kindness, then was blown away by mercy. It was like God was saying, 'I give you mercy, you extend mercy. You can truly trust me to work it out.'" She paused, shaking her head in wonder. "I have to realize that he is supernatural, working outside of time and space, taking care of stuff that seems unreachable."

She smiled. "It inspires me to live in the finished work of Christ. I was so glad that God prepared me before I got there with my client, face-to-face with the ex-coworker. By practicing kindness and mercy these last few weeks, ahead of time, without me really even knowing I would need it—I was able to live and walk and experience soul freedom."

TKM How have you practiced?
What have you learned?

Compassion is the keen awareness of the interdependence of all things.

THOMAS MERTON

DAY 27

Steadfast Joy

> Joy can only be real if people look upon their life as a service and have a definite object in life outside themselves and their personal happiness.
>
> LEO TOLSTOY

In our younger years we do things that seem great in the moment that, years later, reveal themselves to be not so great.

With five kids, lots of cousins, and kids of friends whom I adore, I feel like I get to live those years over by watching people I love wade through the same waters I did. Even though their landscape might look a little different, the currents are the same. So much of which, again, stems from do-and-be-in-order-to-be-okay hurdles. The accumulating, achieving, CrossFitting, Instagramming, striving, Whole30ing, Pinteresting, Snapchatting, TikToking, and harsher drinking, smoking, vaping, etc. (much of which is stuff of today—which will absolutely be obsolete and replaced with something else in the future).

The other night I held my breath as one of my kids waded into waters that, at the onset, seemed harmless but could have easily become a swift current that could take even the strongest people for quite a ride before they could find themselves in need of help to get out.

I tried to speak some wisdom into his heart. "You know that what you're choosing isn't a problem. But please don't buy into any of its message that by doing it you'll fit in or be okay."

"Yeah, I know," he replied. "It's not like I'm doing anything illegal."

You might be wondering what it is my kid was choosing to do. Since every road of life has a few speed bumps along the way, it seems better to leave it open. The issue could be a Bar Method class—a terrific way to stay fit, unless the wall of mirrors trips you into looking at your body and tying your worth to outward aspects of yourself in comparison with others next to you. Or it could be an unassuming beer with friends that makes you feel warm on the inside, possibly numbing pains from the outside world, that easily turns into lots of beers, and more. Or it could be . . . fill in the blank.

"Yes." I agreed. "You're not doing anything illegal. And it's fine. Unless you're doing it to make you okay." I think that's the clincher: doing or having a certain something that will make us okay. "As if it will be the hidden treasure that somehow gives you the peace and joy you've been looking for."

I know those are weird words to say to a kid: *peace* and *joy*. But honestly, that's what the things of this world promise. It's what we all want, so we might as well call it out. Especially since the world's ways give everything *but* lasting peace and joy.

The next day, while pulling a few things together for someone, I bumped into a carpool chat video we had recorded with the team of WayFM's *Wally Show*. They had been in Dallas for a Christmas event and were so kind to get in the car with me to chat about joy. I had asked them to share their tips to leading a joy-filled life. It's my favorite question to ask people.

"First thing," Wally shared, "you have to choose joy. The reality? Joy for me is a lot of times, more often than not, a choice."

He's right. And it's not always easy, especially when we're faced with a parade of what appear to be easier quick fixes to the challenging parts of life.

Wally continued. "If you're looking for negativity in the world, pessimism in the world—you're going to find that. Or it's going to find you." Then he added, "If you're looking for joy or thankfulness, then that's going to find you. Which goes back to you've got to *choose* joy."

Wally suggested grabbing thankfulness as a starter lifeline. I love the consistency between his words and what we've discovered during the Peace Project. We have found thankfulness to be the tried and true on-ramp for igniting good things.

"When you get out of your wallowing and you start being thankful, that helps bring joy. What do you do to get unstuck?" Wally asked. "Start being thankful for *one* thing. One thing every day. Just pray little short prayers, 'Lord, I'm thankful for this.' Even if you're frustrated. Then all of a sudden, you'll find other things to be thankful for. And before you know it, you'll find yourself having short conversations with God throughout the day, which can be transformative."

Becca, another of the show's hosts, shared something from a friend of hers who had lost her sixteen-year-old son to a long health battle. "She told me that not every day is going to be so filled with joy . . . but you can look for that joy. And you're going to find it every single day, even in the hard."

Wally wrapped up our conversation with a terrific exercise that his wife had done at a conference. The leaders asked each participant to look around and pick someone to write a letter to, a note of encouragement. "The leader told the group to write what you think the person needs to know. So they all write it down. Then the twist at the end. The leader said, 'That letter? Don't give it to anybody. That letter? It is for you.'"

We all oohed and nodded at the story. What a great exercise.

"The leader got it," Wally said. "We give everybody the advice, you know: 'that's what you should do.' But we don't internalize it when that same advice is just as applicable to us."[1]

So good.

What secret-tip letter would you write? Who could use an encouraging word today? Something specific that can speak life over the circumstances or situations overwhelming their life? Consider writing it down, maybe let it fill today's gratitude spot in our Peace Project. Then read what you've written as a gift to yourself. Those words just might encourage you today.

Thankfulness spurs joy, and joy spills over into living out kindness and mercy to others as well as ourselves. But all of these things can only go so far when left to us and our own strength.

Lasting joy occurs when we go where the famous hymn written by Isaac Watts in 1719 takes us. Though we sing it at Christmas, it wasn't written as a holiday tune. And its lyrics can encourage any day.

> *Joy to the world* (statement of truth)
> *The Lord is come* (the verb tense conveys power today, yesterday, and every day)
> *The Savior reigns* (victory that literally spans the ages) . . .
>
> *He rules the world with truth and grace,*
> *And makes the nations prove*
> *The glories of his righteousness,*
> *and wonders of his love.*[2]

Think about these words and how they inform all that fills our lives. May the "glories of his righteousness" captivate our thoughts and prompt actions that give life as they are informed by the "wonders of his love" through which we have been unequivocally made right/okay—today and every day.

As I sat with my kid, I couldn't help but add a little extra for good measure.

"You're okay. Today, whether you feel it or not, you've been declared and made okay. You don't have to have that certain job or participate in an activity or wear cool clothes, drive a certain car, or live in a type of house to be okay."

I silently prayed, *Please let him hear those words.* Then I started thinking about the letter-writing exercise Wally described—*the thing you think they need to know.* The thing that I might need to know as well.

"You are okay," I repeated since I can always use a reminder too. "Not according to me. Though there really is nothing you can do or not do to stop my love for you. No, you have been made okay by someone who gave a lot for you simply because you are everything to him."

And I found myself pleading for my son's innermost thoughts: *Please hear the truth. May it drown out all the messages with which the world bombards. Please stop playing the broken records showering you with negative ideas about yourself. Please put on repeat truth and things for which you can be grateful. Please put them into action so that their roots can grow and create new paths and superhighways for thoughts to travel. And give yourself a break. Let go and sink into the joy and peace within reach. Please reach out, grab hold of those truths, and never let go.*

And as I silently said that prayer, I asked that I may breathe it all in for myself as well.

On the way to school, a heavy fog blanketed our drive. I love mornings like those. They're just so beautiful and mysterious.

I mused my thoughts out loud with the boys. "I love the fog. It's just so cool. Every other morning we can see downtown but not today. Whether we can see it or not does not affect the truth that it's there."

"Mahhwmm," one groaned, rolling his eyes.

"No, really. I can't wait to someday ask God if he did things like fog on purpose. You know, like a living-learning experience. Where you're living out an example of something ethereal or heady."

Silence.

It was too early for them, poor things. But not for me. They might not have been moved by the fog, but I was. I lingered down each street, loving the reminders of seeing things in what can't be seen today.

TKM How have you practiced?
What have you learned?

Joy can only be real if people look upon their life as a service and have a definite object in life outside themselves and their personal happiness.

LEO TOLSTOY

DAY 28

Surprise Treasure

> The things you take for granted, someone else is praying for.
>
> MARLAN RICO LEE

Rummaging through one of our kitchen drawers, a scary prospect most any day, I struggled to find the bottle opener. A Topo Chico water bottle was calling my name. Though the opener evaded my search, I did find an unexpected treasure: a thoughtful quote hand-lettered by Snopes.

I love her lettering. But I especially enjoy the quote that crossed her path and warranted a rare card. This one stopped me in my tracks, especially considering our Soul30 journey.

The things you take for granted, someone else is praying for.

The words reminded me to slow down long enough to look for, to see, and to acknowledge life's good, because it's worth seeing and saying rather than taking for granted.

I think that's part of gratitude's power.

So I ticked through things that might not seem like a big deal to me in the moment. Things for which someone else might be praying. I went patriotic as landscapes often set folks questioning. *I'm thankful to live in a country founded upon principles of life and liberty. Thankful for ALL the healthcare and city workers who keep showing up and are endlessly professional and kind. For brave men and women who serve both defending and protecting this country as well as running it and running for office. I'm thankful for all who do it for the greater good, certainly not for the big bucks.*

Ministry leader Shelley Giglio recently posted that "gratitude isn't an emotion; it's a posture."[1] I like that. Thankfulness is an act, a practice that physically feels good and lightens the load. It's worth a pause and shout-out.

So I continued, now thinking of the blessings closest to home. *And I'm grateful for the youngest of our brood taking care of all his stuff, leading the way to the car so we can be on time to the morning carpool.*

Birdie turned to me after dropping off Fury and asked, "Have you ever had that feeling when you feel so good? When you know you're doing exactly what God wants for you?"

"Did that happen to you?" I asked in response.

"It did yesterday," he told me.

"Well what were you doing that made you feel that way?" Seriously, I wanted to know.

He kept his eyes on the road ahead, looking deep in thought. "I can't remember," he said, slow-nodding. "But it felt good whatever that was."

Oh my goodness.

I think that's how we feel when we're connected with the unique purpose and gifting that is literally woven into our soul. It's the essence of our being, what we are made to do. It feels right. And good. And it should never be beholden to any public opinion but should be embraced and held on to as a precious treasure and used for our good and for the good of others.

I think that peace is woven within settling into what God has woven within each of us.

Frederick Buechner adds joy to the same category as the peace that comes with purpose:

> God created us in joy and created us for joy, and in the long run not all the darkness there is in the world and in ourselves can separate us finally from that joy, because whatever else it means to say that God created us in his image, I think it means that even when we cannot believe in him, even when we feel most spiritually bankrupt and deserted by him, his mark is deep within us. We have God's joy in our blood.[2]

Later that day, I looked over at Snopes, who works in the art world. Most creative spheres make it especially challenging to experience peace. It's good to talk about this stuff, to grab perspective.

"Listen," I told her. "Don't let someone else's opinion overinform what you do. Maybe opinions and someone's acting or not acting upon them is actually an opportunity."

"An opportunity?" she repeated. "Yes."

I had been thinking about this and wanted her take. "Maybe opinions trip us up because we need a stumble. It's like a blip or a glitch to catch our attention so that we don't hand over everything based on how we're received by others. Whether or not a like, share, purchase, or whatever else is on the other side shouldn't be the deciding factor. Those things are by-products—not the reason to create."

"Okay," she jumped in, "just thinking out loud here. But what if those things trip us up so that we stop for a second? What if the tripping is actually what helps me focus on what matters? That I'm not doing this for acceptance or achievement; I'm doing it because I love it. I want people to feel encouraged when they see a piece. Because I think it's what I'm created to do." I guess she's been thinking about this too.

"It's like"—she paused to find the right word, or maybe to let it sink in—"it's like a stone of gold. You trip over it, then get to look back and see that the rock that tripped you is actually a beautiful treasure."

I love that word picture. It isn't the success that matters. It's the doing because you're created to do it and do it well out of simple respect for the people involved.

Snopes continued, "It's hard to unlearn the achievement pressures part of doing something well. But to focus on purpose is so freeing. Today I picked up a canvas and started painting just to do it and couldn't believe how good and happy that made me feel." Tapping into gifting and purpose then leaning into the simple joy and freedom that comes with doing what we are created to do is an important part of creating in the first place.

This past weekend I caught an interview with Thomas Heatherwick, an English designer who has been involved in such creations as the Olympic Cauldron for the 2012 Summer Olympics. Recently, he was commissioned for a project in New York's Hudson Yards, the sixteen-building shopping complex on the West Side of Manhattan. Heatherwick's "Vessel" is a giant, 150-foot-tall, honeycomb-like sculpture with 154 staircases for people to climb and descend in the middle of the mall. More than a sculpture, those involved "wanted to make something that everybody could use, touch, and relate to."[3]

When asked about how he will judge it to be a success while awaiting reviews of the inaugural visitors, Heatherwick replied, "Success is a really funny thing." Then he paused. "I suppose we can't predict how people are going to use it. It just . . . is. And then, what happens now has nothing to do with me."[4]

So true. So hard to remember.

Os Guinness, English author and social critic, adds this as it relates to our calling:

> Only madmen, geniuses, and supreme egoists do things purely for themselves. It is easy to buck a crowd, not too hard to march

> to a different drummer. But it is truly difficult—perhaps impossible—to march only to your own drumbeat. Most of us, whether we are aware of it or not, do things with an eye to the approval of some audience or other. The question is not whether we have an audience but which audience we have.
>
> This observation underscores another vital feature of the truth of calling: A life lived listening to the decisive call of God is a life lived before one audience that trumps all others—the Audience of One.[5]

How much better it is to lean in and surrender to our audience of one who always stands with an adoring ovation over our doing well with the gifts he has given us. And in doing so invites us to engage in the more challenging aspects of practicing kindness and mercy—being kind and merciful to ourselves.

Snopes put a cherry on top of her analogy. "If I can just remember to pick up those golden rocks that trip me and keep them as reminders that feelings of unworthiness or insignificance are a waste of time, I can be energized by the fact that I don't have to prove anything because I'm already approved, okay, and good to do what I'm made to do simply because it's who I am."

Amen.

Later that day, I took Mitty on a walk and bumped into some encouragement from our neighborhood sidewalk prophet. She had written,

When life knocks you down, fall forward.

Mitty walked past, but I stopped to look back. I pondered and nodded. Yes—regular life is peppered with falls, which are simply part of walking. But rather than staying flat on your back, fall forward. How? It's what Snopes was describing. Tripping, but not staying down, physically or emotionally. Getting up, not ignoring the fall, but learning from it and moving forward. Because we can.

Why can we? Simply stated in one word: hope. We have hope rooted in solid ground, even when the ground looks unstable or questionable. It's hope that comes from God who, as we've already noted, operates in because/then statements instead of relying on ifs. Because we have been made okay (righteous), we can fall forward, walk free, and sink into the joy and peace that are available even in the stumbles.

TKM How have you practiced?
What have you learned?

The things you take for granted, someone else is praying for.

MARLAN RICO LEE

DAY 29

In It Together

> How beautiful a day can be when kindness touches it.
>
> GEORGE ELLISTON

"Hey, buddy," Snopes and I greeted Birdie as he struggled, sans complaint, to get his backpack and PE bag into the back seat of her little car.

"How was your day?" I asked.

"You know," he said, then paused. "It was great."

Well, that was good to hear. *Great* isn't always the case after a day at middle school.

He hopped inside, and we turned onto the street outside the school. Construction had been the name of the game for several weeks. Going both ways, work trucks commandeered one of the two lanes on a street that has never been a stranger to stacked cars. The lanes were lined with large orange-and-white cones that created a lengthier wait than normal.

A wait that was a bit too long for a car in front of us.

We all watched as a mom with a carful of little kids just out of school took the opportunity to U-turn and try an alternate route. Sadly she didn't see the work cone directly in her path. Sturdy, but pliable, the cone attached itself to the underside of her SUV, so as she drove by us, the cone dragged with her.

"Oh my goodness." We empathetically giggled. Been there, done that.

"I don't think it's going to come off," Snopes said with a look of worry on her face. "She's going to have to back up to get it off."

By this point, realizing that something was dragging under her car, the mom had pulled over. Standstill stuck in the line of traffic, we watched as she got out of the car, looked at the cone, bent down and tried to pull it out, failed, then got down on her hands and knees and started tugging—unsuccessfully.

"We should help her," Snopes said, commiserating with the woman.

"Done!" I followed an opening in the line of traffic and repeated the stuck mom's U-turn.

"Wait." Snopes gasped, rethinking her suggestion. "I didn't mean for you to turn around."

"No, you're right," I said. "There is no way she will get that thing out from under her car." With Soul30 in mind, we took on the kindness opportunity.

We pulled over in front of her car. And Snopes cringed, then jumped out with a cheerful smile. "Can I help?"

We could hear the little kids in her car moaning in embarrassment. Been there, done that too.

Snopes stood next to the mom. "Why don't I grab the cone while you back up your car? I think it will come off."

"Sounds good to me." The mom accepted her help, sighing with a little relief as she hopped into her car. The kids were silent, probably not sure what was going on.

The mom put the car in reverse and slowly backed up. A few crunchy sounds came from the bottom of her car, punctuated by squeals from within. Snopes held tight, then triumphantly pointed to the dislodged cone. Sounds of cheering erupted from the back seat of her SUV.

We cracked up.

Little hands waved out the windows as cheers blanketed their getaway. Then we followed them, pulled out, and got back in the line of traffic.

After a few minutes, Snopes looked over at me. "Gosh, I feel so good. Like, physically good."

"That's what kindness does. It makes everyone feel good," I singsong-nodded.

She smirked with a slight eye roll.

I know they get tired of me, but pointing out the actual physical euphoria resulting from practicing kindness is worth doing. And it's not a momentary jolt. That feeling lingers. We didn't know the mom. We didn't exchange names. The only verbal exchanges were the cute kid-cheers. It was a quick stop. And the only cost, outside of five minutes at most, were a few specks of dirt on Snopes's pants from getting on the ground to dislodge the cone.

But that one minor cost was far outshined by the reward of everyone walking away encouraged.

Acting out kindness is an easy way to give a blessing to another. Kindness for kindness' sake, not so someone will see your action and do something for you in return. And there's something about practicing kindness and mercy *together* that must not go unsaid or unnoticed. Because we really are in this walk of life together.

We can easily lose sight of our commonality for so many reasons—differences in life stages, experiences, nationalities, socioeconomic histories, education, languages, or simply our backgrounds. Our common thread, the humanness of us all being created in the image of God, should never be overlooked.

There are times when a great equalizer comes on the scene. Like the COVID-19 pandemic that leveled every playing field, taking life to the studs across the world. The pandemic opened eyes to our common core, as well as opportunities to connect in everyday situations. In the midst of massive heartache, uncertainty, and hardship, silver linings—most of which centered on human connectedness and interaction (helping each other and banding together)—also showed up around the world.

We've had an influx of opportunities to be kind. They've put fuel in lots of empty tanks. And they connect us.

I saw it show up at the grocery store as an angry person before me in the checkout line barked at the bagger. Something was wrong, but instead of returning the rude words, the bagger respectfully fixed whatever happened and the person moved on. And, rather than sharing an eye roll or gossiping about the rude, the bagger and checker nodded kindly at each other. "These are hard days for everyone," the checker gently said to me.

The power of kindness cannot be overstated. It defies mathematical logic where subtraction (giving away) equals less. But with kindness, giving away equals more and even multiplies our joy. Practicing kindness gives back. And it gives us a break from ourselves as our eyes turn outward.

ALONGSIDE

GRATITUDE: Perspective Power-Pack

I'm often trying to pull myself out of my moments so I can see beyond to what good is happening.

Which might be why gratitude is so helpful. It helps us to see perspective in the moment.

—KM—

TKM How have you practiced?
What have you learned?

How beautiful a day can be when kindness touches it.

GEORGE ELLISTON

DAY 30

Peace

> Wherever there is a human being, there is an opportunity for a kindness.
>
> LUCIUS ANNAEUS SENECA

On my way to meet a couple of my Peace Project friends for coffee after carpool drop-off, I turned down a street and spotted a dog meandering through front yards. He looked a tiny bit disheveled and a little lost. But it was hard to tell. He could have been on his own block, checking out the neighbors' yards.

I passed him, then decided to circle the block to be sure. By the time I made my way back to the street where I first saw him, he was still meandering, definitely lost.

So I stopped and got out of my car to try to call him over. He came close, then playfully darted out of reach. I looked up the street, saw a woman with her dogs, and noticed she was heading our way. Then another gal with her dog joined our puppy posse. Together we wrangled the wandering dog and calls were made. And while we were out there, yet another kind neighbor, in whose yard we were standing, came out of her house. She offered to put

Bo, the tired but still rowdy white Pyrenees who had sweetly shared his muddy paw prints and shed hair on my clothes, in her back yard until the relieved owner came to retrieve him.

Kindness.

Sometimes it's simple. Sometimes it's dirty. But it's always special, and it's extra special when together. Even with people you don't know.

I was thankful for such nice people who saw a problem, stopped, and worked together to solve it.

I shared the story with my friends.

"The coolest part—there was no judgment. Nothing against the owner for leaving their gate open or for having a rowdy dog that was two miles away from home. I loved that." I thought about it and our entire thirty-day pilgrimage. "*And*—and this has been the case with every single opportunity upon which we have acted—a little kindness and thankfulness can make the whole day great. We all felt terrific. I think because it's soul good."

"Yes, soul good," Bev said, nodding.

"Mercy has been it for me," Nan chimed in. "Not that it has been easy."

"I can write out gratitude and find opportunities to be kind," she continued, "but I have struggled with writing down ways to do mercy. And I've wondered why. I've even talked to my daughter about it. Because when we connect with mercy, it's almost magical."

Our friend Jo spoke up. "I know. For me, mercy really has packed a punch. It's fascinating to consider the power of mercy."

I completely agree. I think it's because mercy can't be just a human effort. It really occurs at the soul-level. We can physically go through the motions of being kind or writing down things for which we are thankful, but mercy goes to the core, to our innermost being. And we can't seem to genuinely connect with mercy in and of our own strength alone.

"Mercy is supernatural," Bev said, "which is why it's great. But that's probably also why it's a challenge. Seeing as surrender is in it too." She paused, then added, "Yes. But surrender *in*, not surrender *to*, which is a big difference."

"Wow," I replied. "It's not *handing* ourselves over to someone's chaos—though I love the *chaos* descriptor—but *surrendering* that's more like sinking into God's mercy that somehow flows from the source." I paused. "Yeah . . . sort of, it's hard to describe."

"I'm glad it's not just me." Jo laughed. "This morning, I went to the store before coming here. Of course, someone was going super slow in the parking lot. I thought, *I could zoom around them and be really angry. Or I could choose to wait and wait and wait.* So I chose to wait, with a peaceful heart, which I'm not sure I would or could have done thirty days ago."

Why is mercy always in the car? I laughed with her. Maybe for me because I'm always in it!

"I've realized that mercy is just making a different connection," Jo continued. "Because, rather than get angry, mercy moves me to ask, *Are they lost*? *Or having a bad day*? *Or just lingering and enjoying their day?* And here's where it hits me—what I am finding out is that mercy connects me to humanity."

I'll say that again since it bears repeating. Mercy connects us to humanity. Wow.

Jo didn't stop there. "So then I reflect back on myself too. Kind of thinking about when I feel like I don't want to be merciful, and I ask myself, Why is that? Because I'm having a bad day or I'm upset with myself? Or is it because I feel bad about myself? And so everything comes full circle. I realize right there that we're in it together. Yes, mercy connects me to humanity, to others, and to *myself*."

There's something about mercy. It sees people, not for what they've done but for who they are: humans.

Mercy is seeing beyond a moment to the person.

Mercy's compassion ignites an idea. Willingness puts the idea into soul-level action. And kindness, spurred by gratitude, offers practical action points of doing. It helps us to see and to treat people as God does, as humans of great worth. It calls perspective into the conversation. Mercy reaches deep, moving our actions from surface-level to the heart. Maybe that's why our souls, our innermost beings, have been so deeply impacted by this exercise.

Mercy dials down all the what-ifs and the iterations that can race through our thoughts as we try to fix situations gone bad. Mercy walks through the door that's opened by the practices of thankfulness and kindness, where our eyes cannot be anchored on ourselves. And once on the other side, mercy pours out peace like ointment into wounds, binding the broken parts and breathing life into all that threatens to steal it.

Mercy stills the storms.

I find myself revisiting the definition of mercy as a constant reminder. Thinking back on Oxford Dictionary's definition of mercy, "a kind or forgiving attitude toward someone that you have the power to harm or the right to punish" (even ourselves), and adding it again to the definition given by James Keenan: "willingness to enter into the chaos of another." Both definitions show that mercy thrives on forgiveness and compassion.

Saint Francis of Assisi called mercy "a heart sensitive to misery . . . that which seemed bitter to me was changed into sweetness of soul and body." For Mother Teresa, mercy in action "was the 'salt' which gave flavor to her work, it was the 'light which shone in the darkness of the many who no longer had tears to shed for their poverty and suffering.'"[1] For me, I think mercy is narrowing down to the willingness to compassionately consider and proactively meet someone where they are, whether in thought or deed.

It invites daily opportunities to slow down, to breathe, and to see beyond a moment to the people involved, especially when coupled with thankfulness and acts of kindness. May we grab hold more often and hang on longer, meeting people where they are with compassion and loving people for who they are.

One of the things we have absolutely experienced in our practicing thankfulness, kindness, and mercy is the peace permeating in and perpetuated through the action point of doing these three things. Not just thinking about them but doing them as well: writing down things to be thankful for, practicing kindness, extending mercy to others and to ourselves. It's like winning a trifecta.

I think peace comes as these actions set us free from, well, from ourselves.

Our hands are quite literally pried away from so many things we can't stop ourselves from hanging onto, even though, by grace God has set us free from them. Things like expectations, anxieties, fears, worries, achievements, judgments, resentments, tough circumstances, the things we think we have to do or be in order to be okay.

I shared what my friends and I had discussed with Snopes when I got home that evening.

"It's like living a fairy tale," Snopes said. "You know that the glass slipper fits and the downtrodden, mistreated maiden is actually royalty. Except this is better. Because it's real."

I think she's right; it's almost too good to be true. And it's all about the grace and freedom, regardless of our station in life, that come from a source that never fails us.

"You know," she continued, "it may be hard to stay the course and keep leaning into this new freedom, but I'm sure going to try. I'm so thankful we don't have to go it alone. By myself, I'm sure I would forget."

"Me too."

Thank goodness we never need travel our life road alone either. I thought about that as I headed out the door for afternoon pickup. I backed out of our driveway, thankful for the morning standoff that started our thankfulness, kindness, and mercy journey.

And on the final day of Soul30, the not-alone piece might have been my biggest point of gratitude. I'm so thankful to be traveling next to people—some friends, some strangers—but all people of great worth who matter. I'm *thankful* to be traveling the road next to my kids, especially. *Mercy* has barreled in, helping with the days when junior high insecurity still shows up. Thankfulness sits ever-ready and available to salvage the day. And I'm thankful for the opportunities to practice *kindness*.

Birdie got in the car. He's an easy target for kindness.

"How about some popcorn?" I asked.

"That would be nice," he sigh-replied, probably feeling blah about an afternoon of homework after a long day of school. "And maybe a Starbucks?"

What?! That's too much! "Sure," I happily agreed. Fifth kid, beyond golden child, it's the platinum spot to be.

He ran in to both places, returning from the theater with excitement that he got to see Anthony again and excitement from his Starbucks trip, where the super nice barista wrote a hello note on the drink he got for his sister. Even in his middle school funk, kindness steadied the ride.

Guess who got you Starbucks, he texted Snopes. Or, at least, he thought he was texting her.

"Wait a minute!" he exclaimed. "Do you group text?"

"What?" I replied.

"Do you have texts with a group of friends?"

"Sure." I shrugged. *Doesn't everyone?*

"Well, I just group-messaged your friends about Starbucks," he said, a bit flustered. "I didn't mean to. I thought I was texting Snopes. Ugh . . . yet another stupid thing today."

"My goodness, that's so not stupid," I reassured him. "I'll just let them know it was a goof. I promise it doesn't matter. We all do it. Which is usually nice to know that we're not alone in our mishaps, even incredibly minor ones like that." Easy mercy.

His practicing kindness was greeted with the sweetest "*YOU GOT THAT FOR ME?!*" from a surprised and touched sister when we got home.

To be remembered is special any day. Because we *are* all in this together.

Thanks for walking the road with me.

ALONGSIDE

MERCY: Together

Mercy just might be the deepest human touchpoint we have with each other: the place where we will connect in eternity. It's safe, life-giving, and life sharing. It is the essence of loving your neighbor AND yourself.

It's not easy, which is probably why gratitude and kindness join the effort.

Practicing these has refreshed me in places I never knew could need refreshing.

May this actually be our new normal.

—Anonymous (which means all of us)—

TKM How have you practiced?
What have you learned?

Wherever there is a human being, there is an opportunity for a kindness.

LUCIUS ANNAEUS SENECA

Acknowledgments

I want to start by thanking you (reader) for picking up this book. Thank you for kindly sharing your time with me, my kids, and a few brave friends who thought that a Soul30 Challenge sounded interesting. I hope this story encourages you, in your day and in your circumstances, toward the hope and peace that is available to each of us. And I hope that you might be inspired to try it out yourself, even if only for a few days.

A very special and heartfelt thank-you to Andrea Doering. Thank you for brainstorming with me, for endlessly encouraging me, and for gently meeting me where I am, especially as we travel an unexpected and profoundly difficult road of late. Thank you, Robin Turici, for all the great catches and for smoothing out the rough edges. Thanks also to Eileen Hanson, Melanie Burkhart, Kelli Smith, Patti Brinks, Erin Bartels, Brian Brunsting, and all the Revell sales team for your amazing creativity, fun ideas, and all the hard work and commitment you've put into this book.

Thanks to Wolgemuth & Associates for walking alongside and ahead of me for the last decade. A special thanks to Erik Wolgemuth for your friendship and all the many ways you inspire me and so many people.

Thanks to my friends who stepped up to actually take the Soul30 Challenge during our Neighborhood Studies Jan-Term and for letting me share our journey: Connie, Brenda, Candy, Margaret, Suzanne, Tiffany, Cheryl, Chrissy, Darian, Nancy, Laura D, Lisa, Hillary, Allison, Laura T, Lori, Jacky, Lindsey, Billye, Johanna, Shirley, Julie, Lindsay, Ann, Claire, Amy, Becky, Susan, Alyssa, Michael, Miriam, Judy C, Maggie, Judy F, Alison, and Natalie. I'm humbled by your willingness to jump on board an idea and make it such an honest/authentic reality. Thanks to all my *MOATblog*, *SaySomethingShow*, and Neighborhood Studies friends who have walked the road with me over the years—it sure would be a lonely adventure without you!

A special thank-you to Ron, Holley, Leon, Melissa, Susie, Melanie, Heather, Scott, Brenda, and Kristin for reading and lending your name to this project. I'm grateful and humbled, to say the least.

My absolute biggest thank-you to Jon and especially our kids. I'd rather spend time with you than any people on this planet. I love you. I'm inspired by you. I'm a better person for knowing you. Thanks for putting up with and being a part of my silly ideas.

If there is any truth or wisdom in this book, it isn't mine. I'm just along for the ride. All wisdom within is supplied by the Author of Truth. He has so much more to share and gives generously without finding fault (see James 1:5). Check it out sometime. We read the New International Version (1984) around our house.

Notes

Introduction

1. Matthew 22:37–39.

2. Oxford Learner's Dictionary, s.v. "mercy," accessed October 5, 2020, https://www.oxfordlearnersdictionaries.com/us/definition/american_english/mercy.

3. Daniela Silva, "Kindness and Brain: What Is the Impact of Kindness in Brain Functioning?" EC Neurology Conceptual Paper, March 28, 2017, https://www.ecronicon.com/ecne/pdf/ECNE-05-00135.pdf.

4. Julie Hani, "The Neuroscience of Behavior Change," StartUp Health, August 8, 2017, https://healthtransformer.co/the-neuroscience-of-behavior-change-bcb567fa83c1.

Day 1 Thankfulness: A Nice Place to Start

1. Paul J. Mills, "A Grateful Heart Is a Healthier Heart," American Psychological Association, April 9, 2015, https://www.apa.org/news/press/releases/2015/04/grateful-heart.

2. Anna Hart, "Gratitude: The Latest Self-Help Trend That Could Change Your Life," *Telegraph*, July 4, 2015, https://www.telegraph.co.uk/women/womens-health/11706352/Gratitude-the-latest-self-help-trend-that-could-change-your-life.html.

Day 2 Be Brave, Be Kind

1. Steve Hartman, "Boy Enamored with the American Flag Gets His Own Spot to Appreciate Its Beauty," CBS News, August 2, 2019, https://www.cbsnews.com/news/finn-daly-american-flag-todd-disque-builds-bench-for-boy-to-look-at-flag/.

2. J. R. Thorpe, "Being Nice to Someone Literally Makes Your Brain Light Up, Science Says," Bustle, October 12, 2018, https://www.bustle.com/p/how-kindness-changes-your-brain-according-to-new-research-12079120.

3. Thorpe, "Being Nice to Someone."

4. University of Sussex, "The Warm Glow of Kindness Is Real—Sussex Study Confirms," EurekAlert!, September 27, 2018, https://www.eurekalert.org/pub_releases/2018-09/uos-twg092718.php.

5. "The Positive Effects of Kindness on Our Mental Health," AIFC, January 23, 2008, https://www.aifc.com.au/positive-kindness-mental-health/.

6. Scott Mautz, "Science Says 'Random Acts of Kindness' Week Has Astonishing Health Benefits," *Inc.*, February 13, 2017, https://www.inc.com/scott-mautz/science-says-random-acts-of-kindness-week-has-astonishing-health-benefits.html.

Day 3 Mysterious Mercy

1. Oxford Learner's Dictionary, s.v. "mercy," accessed October 5, 2020, https://www.oxfordlearnersdictionaries.com/us/definition/american_english/mercy.

2. As quoted in Kerry Weber, *Mercy in the City: How to Feed the Hungry, Give Drink to the Thirsty* (Chicago: Loyola Press, 2014), 12.

3. Dr. Edith Eva Eger, *The Choice: Embrace the Possible* (New York: Scribner, 2017), 41.

4. Exodus 34:6.

5. Francis of Assisi, *The Testament*, in *Francis of Assisi: Early Documents*, ed. R. J. Armstrong, J. A. W. Hellman, and W. J. Short, vol. 1, *The Saint* (New York: New City Press, 1999), 124.

6. Brian Purfield, "Francis of Assisi: A Channel of Mercy," *Thinking Faith*, September 30, 2016, https://www.thinkingfaith.org/articles/francis-assisi-channel-mercy#_edn1.

7. Purfield, "Francis of Assisi."

Day 5 Mercy's Soul Sightings

1. "The Importance of Connection - Dr Chi Chi Obuaya - HTB at Home," YouTube video, posted by HTB Church, 2:00, April 19, 2020, https://www.youtube.com/watch?v=LHLZM7sKVd8.

2. As quoted in Justin Taylor, "Apocryphal Quote from C. S. Lewis on the Soul and the Body," *The Gospel Coalition* (blog), July 5, 2012, https://www.thegospelcoalition.org/blogs/justin-taylor/apocryphal-quote-from-c-s-lewis-on-the-soul-and-the-body/.

3. "SaySomething Show: Sally Lloyd-Jones, New Book and Wise Tips," YouTube video, posted by Kay Wyma, 26:23, May 17, 2018, https://youtu.be/O5MglTaXJm4.

Day 6 Our Identity

1. Janna Koretz, "What Happens When Your Career Becomes Your Whole Identity?," *Harvard Business Review*, December 26, 2019, https://hbr.org/2019/12

/what-happens-when-your-career-becomes-your-whole-identity?utm_source=pocket-newtab.

2. Gregg Henriques, "The Core Need," *Psychology Today*, June 25, 2014, https://www.psychologytoday.com/us/blog/theory-knowledge/201406/the-core-need.

3. "U. S. Senate Chaplain Dr. Barry Black Full Remarks at National Prayer Breakfast (C-SPAN)," YouTube video, posted by C-SPAN, February 2, 2017, https://www.youtube.com/watch?v=zyvNg1kk9tQ.

Day 7 Mindsight Isn't 20/20

1. Kendra Cherry, "What is the Negativity Bias?," *Very Well Mind*, updated April 29, 2019, https://www.verywellmind.com/negative-bias-4589618.

2. "SaySomething: Lysa TerKeurst on Tackling Rejection," YouTube video, posted by Kay Wyma, August 29, 2016, https://www.youtube.com/watch?v=f91SWVblOAg.

3. "SaySomething: Lysa TerKeurst."

4. Dallas Willard, *The Divine Conspiracy* (San Francisco: HarperCollins, 1998), 324.

5. Charles Swindoll, *The Grace Awakening* (Nashville: Thomas Nelson, 1990).

Day 10 Mercy's Compassion

1. "Contemplating Kindness with Leon Logothetis Host of The Kindness Diaries," YouTube video, posted by Kay Wyma, May 12, 2017, https://www.youtube.com/watch?v=zW8h9b0o1mM.

2. Emma Seppälä, "Doctors Who Are Kind Have Healthier Patients Who Heal Faster, According to New Book," *Washington Post*, April 29, 2019, https://www.washingtonpost.com/lifestyle/2019/04/29/doctors-who-show-compassion-have-healthier-patients-who-heal-faster-according-new-book/.

Day 11 Mercy's Forgiveness

1. "Brandt Jean to Amber Guyger: 'I Forgive You,'" YouTube video, posted by ABC News, October 2, 2019, https://www.youtube.com/watch?v=NkoE_GQsbNA.

2. John S. Dickerson, "Charleston Victims Wield Power of Forgiveness: Column," *USA Today*, June 21, 2015, https://www.usatoday.com/story/opinion/2015/06/21/charleston-church-shooting-families-forgiveness-column/29069731/.

3. June Hunt, "June Hunt on Forgiveness: The Freedom of Forgiveness," Hope for the Heart Ministries, April 2017, https://www.hopefortheheart.org/june-hunt-on-forgiveness-the-freedom-of-forgiveness/.

4. Tony Evans, "The Freedom of Forgiveness," *Tony Evans: The Urban Alternative* (blog), accessed October 1, 2020, https://tonyevans.org/the-freedom-of-forgiveness/.

5. Tony Evans, "Two Types of Forgiveness," Authentic Manhood, April 13, 2018, https://www.authenticmanhood.com/two-types-of-forgiveness/.

Day 13 The Willingness of Mercy

1. Corrie ten Boom, "Guideposts Classics: Corrie ten Boom on Forgiveness," Guideposts, posted on July 24, 2014, https://www.guideposts.org/better-living/positive-living/guideposts-classics-corrie-ten-boom-on-forgiveness.
2. Ten Boom, "Guideposts Classics."
3. Ten Boom, "Guideposts Classics."
4. Ten Boom, "Guideposts Classics."
5. Brian Stevenson, *Just Mercy: A Story of Justice and Redemption* (New York: Random House, 2014), 289.
6. Henri Nouwen, *Life of the Beloved: Spiritual Living in a Secular World* (New York: The Crossroad Publishing Company, 1992), 21.

Day 15 A Person's Chaos

1. Michael J. Formica, "What Sort of Chaos Do You Invite?" *Psychology Today*, January 21, 2011, https://www.psychologytoday.com/us/blog/enlightened-living/201101/what-sort-chaos-do-you-invite.
2. Formica, "What Sort of Chaos."

Day 16 Kindness without Consequence

1. Dr. Kent M. Keith, "The Paradoxical Commandments," accessed November 13, 2020, http://www.paradoxicalcommandments.com/index.html.
2. Tony Fahkry, "How the Power of Kindness Impacts Your Life and Others," Mission.org, December 25, 2017, https://medium.com/the-mission/how-the-power-of-kindness-impacts-your-life-and-others-f8f5a895400.

Day 18 Keeping It Simple

1. "Many Americans Are Lonely, and Gen Z Most of All, Study Finds," CBS News, May 3, 2018, https://www.cbsnews.com/news/many-americans-are-lonely-and-gen-z-most-of-all-study-finds/.
2. Lee Cowen, "Reaching Out: How Caring Letters Help in Suicide Prevention," *CBS Sunday Morning*, January 19, 2020, https://www.cbsnews.com/news/reaching-out-how-caring-letters-help-in-suicide-prevention/.
3. Cowen, "Reaching Out."
4. "The Queen's Christmas Broadcast 2019," YouTube video, posted by The Royal Family, 4:47, December 25, 2019, https://www.youtube.com/watch?v=HD5oZDKqJWs.

Day 19 Words

1. "Poet & Author Amena Brown on Fixing Our Broken-Record Self Messaging," YouTube video, posted by Kay Wyma, November 11, 2017, https://www.youtube.com/watch?v=NoOocNnevTU.
2. Mary Ann Pietzker, *Miscellaneous Poems* (London, UK: Griffith and Farran, 1872). Public domain.

Day 20 Getting to Why

1. Beyond Blue, "Dan Baker's Six Happiness Tools," Beliefnet, accessed September 28, 2020, https://www.beliefnet.com/columnists/beyondblue/2007/06/dan-bakers-six-happiness-tools.html.

2. Martha Beck, "The Key to Healing Emotional Wounds," Oprah.com, accessed September 28, 2020, http://www.oprah.com/inspiration/martha-beck-how-to-heal-emotional-wounds#ixzz6BfQrqhs2.

3. Beck, "Key to Healing."

4. Beck, "Key to Healing."

Day 21 Deep Well of Grace

1. Keith Beaslye-Topliffe, ed., *Writings of Augustine* (Nashville, TN: Upper Room Books, 2017).

2. Frederick Buechner, *Listening to Your Life* (New York: HarperCollins, 1992), 289.

3. Buechner, *Listening*, 289.

Day 22 Because/Then Statements

1. Lamentations 3:22–23.
2. Isaiah 43:4.
3. 2 Peter 1:3.
4. 2 Timothy 2:13.
5. Zechariah 4:6.
6. Isaiah 43:1 NLT.

Day 23 Settled Significance

1. Linda and Charlie Bloom, "Playing Out Our Childhood Role," *Psychology Today*, December 5, 2017, https://www.psychologytoday.com/us/blog/stronger-the-broken-places/201712/playing-out-our-childhood-role.

Day 25 Judgment and Mercy

1. "Pope Francis at Mass: Imitate the Mercy of the Lord," Vatican News, March 18, 2019, https://www.vaticannews.va/en/pope-francis/mass-casa-santa-marta/2019-03/pope-francis-homily-mass-santa-marta-mercy-lord.html.

2. "Pope Francis at Mass."

3. Victor Frankl, *Man's Search for Meaning* (New York: Hachette, 1979), 44.

Day 27 Steadfast Joy

1. "Wally Show Shares Some History, Laughs & Tips on a Joy," YouTube video, posted by Kay Wyma, December 7, 2018, https://youtu.be/KX6wTP7FhBA.

2. Isaac Watts, "Joy to the World! The Lord Is Come," Hymnary.com, accessed September 28, 2020, https://hymnary.org/text/joy_to_the_world_the_lord_is_come.

Day 28 Surprise Treasure

1. Shelley Giglio, Instagram post on September 22, 2020, https://www.instagram.com/p/CFcAyTKlP3s/.

2. Frederick Buechner, "The Great Dance," in *Secrets in the Dark: A Life in Sermons* (2007; repr., Grand Rapids: HarperCollins, 2006), 240.

3. "The Vessel: Thomas Heatherwick's Oversized Public Art Structure," YouTube video, posted by *CBS Sunday Morning*, March 17, 2019, https://www.youtube.com/watch?v=Gy4Sg6cWGgc.

4. "The Vessel."

5. Os Guinness, *The Call: Finding and Fulfilling the Central Purpose of Your Life* (Nashville: Thomas Nelson, 2003).

Day 30 Peace

1. "Saint Mother Teresa: Dispenser of Divine Mercy," Vatican News, September 4, 2018, https://www.vaticannews.va/en/vatican-city/news/2018-09/mother-teresa-mercy-canonization.html.

Kay Wyma is a mom, blogger, vodcaster, and author of four books in which she has tackled, with candor and humor, some of the troubling societal issues that impact us all. Kay's writings have led her to appearances on *TODAY*, CNN, Hallmark's *Home & Family*, and more. Before staying at home with her kids, she held positions at the White House and Bank of America. She lives in Dallas, Texas, with her husband and five kids. Connect with Kay at kaywyma.com.

GET TO KNOW
KAY!

Head to **kaywyma.com** to learn more about Kay's writing and media appearances or to contact her!

Follow Kay on social media:

kaywyma

themoatblog

Kay Wills Wyma

Kay Wyma